Ramblin' On My Mind

Ramblin' On My Mind

Kent DuChaine

Ramblin' On My Mind

Copyright © 2020

ISBN: 978-1-946702-42-5

All rights reserved. No part of this book may be reproduced or transmitted in any form or by any means, electronic or mechanical, including photocopying, recording, or by any information storage and retrieval system, without permission in writing from the author.

Freeze Time Media

Cover photos courtesy Tim Spencer

This book is dedicated to all the blues cats from the past and to all the hard-working musicians out there following their passion.

Acknowledgments

I want to thank Johnny Shines for taking me under his wing and bringing me along for the final leg of the blues journey he set out on with Robert Johnson so many years ago.

Many thanks to John Morgan for all the help throughout my musical career.

Thank you to Scott Duncan for the friendship and the fantastic foreword.

I want to thank Tim Spencer for the excellent photographs he allowed us to use.

And thanks to Cal Woodard and Shane Sasser for helping me put the book together.

Contents

Foreword	xi
Introduction: A Profound Evening	xv
Childhood in Minnesota	1
Early Adulthood Travels	11
The Northwoods and First Solo Gigs	19
Skin and Bones Take Colorado and New Orleans	27
Ramblin' Around the Gulf Coast and the Keys	35
My Time with Johnny Shines	45
Life on the Lake and Overseas	57
University of Minnesota Blues and Leadbessie	83
Muddy Waters and Stevie Ray Vaughan	91
The Life of "Luxury"	97
Lazy Bill Lucas	111
Howlin' Wolf in Concert	115
More on Europe	119
The Women in My Life	123

Foreword

Kent DuChaine designates the place in Georgia he calls home as "the house the Brits built." It's an apt epithet in more ways than one. For the past 27 years or so, as a solo bluesman, Kent has spent a good part of his blues working life traveling the obscure highways and byways of the United Kingdom of Great Britain and Northern Ireland. Although he has many dedicated fans both in his native United States and in other parts of Europe, I think it's fair to say that it's the UK that has most firmly grasped this dedicated traveling bluesman to its collective bosom.

Kent was first scheduled to play in the UK way back in April 1992. The Gloucester Blues Festival had booked Johnny Shines to headline the festival. In 1989, having relocated to Alabama to immerse himself deeply in the land where blues began, Kent struck up a relationship with the legendary Johnny "Ned" Shines, a one-time traveling companion of the even more legendary King of the Delta Blues, Robert Johnson.

Mr. Shines suffered a stroke in 1980, making it difficult for him to sing and play guitar. Not surprisingly, on this account, his career had come to something of a standstill. However, Kent encouraged Mr. Shines to pick up the guitar again and get back out on the road and play.

With Kent's help and support, Mr. Shines went from strength to strength. As Kent told Britain's Blueprint magazine in June 1992, "We [had] worked maybe 150 shows in 18 months up to that point, and he was strong. I could see it, see him getting stronger. I'd push him four, five nights a week. Sometimes we'd do 10 or 11 shows in a row. Sometimes he'd just come out and play, and I'd be panting trying to keep up with him!"

Kent's efforts in helping Johnny Shines rediscover his chops culminated in the recording of 1991's W.C. Handy Award-winning album Back to the Country. The album sparked renewed interest in Mr. Shines, particularly outside the USA in the UK and other European countries.

Sadly, however, on April 20, 1992, Johnny Shines passed away before he and Kent could perform at the aforementioned Gloucester Blues Festival. Despite this setback, it was nonetheless a new beginning in the career of the itinerant Delta bluesman Kent DuChaine. Although disappointed at not being able to play the Gloucester show with Johnny Shines, Kent returned to the UK in 1993 and played solo at the Gloucester and Burnley Blues Festivals to high acclaim. From these two initial gigs began an annual touring schedule that has seen Kent play all over the UK in cities, towns, villages, and tiny hamlets spread the length and breadth of the British archipelago. It can be a punishing schedule, but Kent's dedication to spreading the word of the blues knows no bounds.

I once went on a nightmare drive with Kent from Portsmouth on the south coast of England to his next gig on the island of Orkney off the north coast of Scotland, a distance of some 755 miles. Included free of charge was a five-hour hold-up in traffic just outside Stoke-on-Trent in England's West Midlands. Needless to say, despite these frustrations, Kent delivered a spectacular show in Orkney—and even found time, while on the island, to indulge in his other great passion: fishing. Not for nothing does he style himself "The Fishing Musician."

It's appropriate that Kent has built such a rapport with British audiences. It's no secret that the UK and the USA have long had a close musical association in terms of the blues. As British author Bob Brunning puts it in his seminal book, Blues in Britain: "There is a strong, almost overwhelming,

Ramblin' On My Mind

argument to be made in support of the oft-aired theory that the huge influx of white R&B bands into the States during the 1960s and 1970s actually directed the American audiences' attention towards their own rich Black blues culture, of which many young white (and Black) Americans were quite unaware. British bands like the Rolling Stones, Cream, Ten Years After, the Yardbirds, Fleetwood Mac, Savoy Brown, John Mayall, and many other groups toured the States with their exciting stage shows, dominated by their fervent and energetic interpretations of the Back rhythm and blues material upon which they all relied. The British musicians involved were quick to credit their American heroes during their stage announcements, press and television interviews, and through their choice of material for albums. Thus, a huge section of the young American concertgoing population began to search out and examine the work of the authentic, original Black artists performing in their own backyard."

A young Kent DuChaine was one of those caught up in this enthusiasm. Regarding his initial interest in the blues, as Kent recounted to Blueprint magazine: "I started listening to this kind of music through the British people, actually. [Eric] Clapton doing 'Crossroads,' 'Rambling on my Mind,' Cream, The Doors, [Jimi] Hendrix. Having heard these songs, [...] I went to the library and asked if they had any records by Robert Johnson. They had the CBS album, [King of the Delta Blues Singers] Volume 1. [...] started listening and it was magical."

And the rest, as they say, is history…

It's been my privilege to have been Kent DuChaine's friend for almost 30 years. Over that time, I must have seen dozens of shows of his both in the UK and the USA. His one constant companion on the road is his battered National Duolian guitar. He calls his guitar LeadBessie, a conflation of the names of two of his blues heroes (of which there are, of course, too many to list here). In this case, folk-blues giant

Huddie Ledbetter and the woman known by the soubriquet, the Empress of the Blues—Bessie Smith. Despite the peaks and troughs of the blues life to which Kent is dedicated, it would be fair to say that LeadBessie is the one "old lady" who has stood by him over the years.

Kent and LeadBessie have had a lot of adventures together. Many are shared in this book. More insight can be gotten by and catching Kent and LeadBessie at a gig somewhere. Kent is on the road often, maintaining the tradition of the itinerant solo bluesman that began way back when in the Mississippi Delta by legendary figures like Bukka White, David "Honeyboy" Edwards, Johnny Shines and, yes—that most iconic of all bluesmen—Robert Johnson.

Like I say, there's nothing quite like a Kent DuChaine gig. The warmth, wit, and wisdom of the blues is all there in Kent's performances, informed by a reverence for the music and a wealth of experiences garnered in almost (gulp!) 50 years of running the roads. If you're in the unfortunate position of never having been to a Kent DuChaine gig, this book will give you a flavor of what you've been missing. Diehard Kent DuChaine fans will love the ride, too!

Scott Duncan
Editor, Blueprint magazine
August 2019

Introduction:
A Profound Evening

This story took place somewhere in 1988, when I was playing in a band called The Grounders. We had been very interested in classic rock and Southern rock bands like the Allman Brothers, Led Zeppelin, Cream, and bands with a heavy influence in the blues. People like Eric Clapton and the members of Led Zeppelin and the Rolling Stones were English musicians who kind of repackaged American blues music and sold it back to America.

I had been playing guitar for about three or four years in this college band in Tuscaloosa, Alabama. My three bandmates and I were students at the University of Alabama, and we used to play at a club called the Booth. I was 22 years old, and one midweek night, we were out at the Booth.

We walked in, and there was this long-haired guy playing a Gibson L5 guitar, an old-style jazz guitar. He had his guitar case open: a bunch of photos of bluesmen decorated it. He was singing original Delta blues music in the vein of Robert Johnson. In that open guitar case, he was taking tips while he shared little tidbits about the blues and his songs with the audience. He was unlike anything I had ever seen! As I sat and listened to Kent DuChaine for the first time, I became enthralled! My bandmates and I had loved blues music and wanted to learn more. Here was a guy who was living in a camper in a state park, going from town to town, playing blues to earn his living. He was living the life we dreamed about.

Our band had a rented house, and I invited Kent over for dinner one night, thinking that since he was living in a campground, he'd probably like a home-cooked meal. I enjoyed cooking and hoped that providing a good meal would give us a chance to pick his brain, hear his stories, and jam with somebody a lot more experienced than we were. I think we cooked up some fried chicken, mashed potatoes and bread. He must have been starving because he ate a lot of it. After dinner, we drank beer, wine, and who knows what else. We jammed for several hours that night. Later, when Kent began telling us his story about Johnny Shines, we didn't know who Johnny Shines was. He said, "Well, Johnny Shines is one of the last known living men to have played with Robert Johnson, the legendary—almost mythical—bluesman. His music only became popular after he died."

Thinking back, I believe we really had at least heard of Johnny Shines, because we knew of a band called the Kokomo Blues and Johnny Shines. We didn't know much about him, though, so I pulled out a Tuscaloosa phonebook. The town was relatively small, so the phonebook wasn't that big. I went to the white pages, looked Shines up and, sure enough, his number was listed!

We were all amazed at finding Shines in the phone book. Shortly after, Kent called Johnny Shines, went over to his house and made his sales pitch. The two of them ended up touring extensively and playing the blues together. Johnny had had a stroke, and though his voice still sounded razor clear, he couldn't press down on the frets of his guitar very well. It was a good marriage for the two of them, because Kent could play the parts that Johnny couldn't, and Johnny had that fantastic voice.

I guess the rest, as they say, is history. I remember it like it was yesterday because it was a profound event in our young musical lives. Here, we invited an old, traveling blues guy into our home, and, as a result, learned about Johnny Shines. It was a fortuitous night for Kent and Johnny because they hooked up. And, it was a godsend to the blues community because they performed for something like three years together. Kent's career has continued to flourish. It was great to be a small part of Kent DuChaine's history.

Cal Woodard

1
Childhood in Minnesota

My story begins when I was born on April 25, 1951, in Wayzata, a suburb of Minneapolis, Minnesota. My father was Gerald DuChaine, or Gerry as many called him. My mother, Carmen, took care of the home and the children. By the time I turned 5, my mom had four kids around the house. She had her hands full as I had two older brothers, Gerry Jr. and Greg, and a little sister, Holly. My youngest brother, David, came along soon after. Our family could probably best be described as lower middle class.

My father spent his whole life working for the U.S. government. He started working in the CCC Camps (Civilian Conservation Corps) when he was 15 years old during the Great Depression and when things became unbearably tough, he left his home. He went to Utah and built roads up in the wilderness and also worked as a wrangler.

When WWII came along, he became a sailor, a chief petty officer. He and my Uncle Mick were both on a big destroyer called the Quincy when the Japanese blew her in half in one of the battles near the Philippines. The ship sank, and my father and uncle floated around in shark-infested waters for quite a few hours, waiting for the Navy to rescue them. Both survived, though my uncle was in and out of hospitals and became drug dependent for a while because of the morphine they gave him. My father was reassigned to fly airplanes in reconnaissance missions.

When he left the war, Dad started working for the Defense Department as a contractor for Honeywell. He then became an inspector and eventually the head of inspection teams examining the work done at factories that had government contracts. He inspected factories that were building NASA satellites, and I remember him bringing some materials home from one of them. It was an aluminum, papery substance that we never did know what was. He did that work for the remainder of his life.

My father was also active in the naval reserves where he was a chief petty officer with 30 years of service. He flew big helicopters used for sonar surveillance of submarines. He'd go on tour every year for a couple of weeks with the reserves. They'd go to the coasts and practice their sub reconnaissance. The helicopters would drop him and others from town off in a field near where we lived. These huge helicopters would fly in, and I would jump on my dear old dad when he came home. It was big excitement for a young kid!

I think my growing up was pretty typical for a boy in the 1950s. With two brothers that were three and four years older than me, I learned early in life how to be competitive. From my point of view, they had more privileges, and I wanted to get up to their level in everything. Since I shared a room with my sister, I formed a strong connection with her.

My family eventually moved to an area called Plymouth, which was the last real northern town before the countryside turned rural. We moved next to my mother's sister, who had a house full of daughters about the same age as we were. With me, my brothers, and my sister living next to four girls, there was an instant neighborhood without counting any other kids in the area. There was plenty of space to roam around the countryside and to get into trouble, as all kids manage to do. The days were full of both summer and winter games and activities. I learned to skate very well due to the big pond my family had in the backyard and the long Minnesota winters.

My progression from elementary school to junior high to high school was pretty normal, I guess. Kids tried to establish a pecking order based on age, size, or neighborhood. I brought the competitive spirit that I'd developed from dealing with my two older brothers into school. When I started kindergarten, I decided to assert my domination over the class bully on the very first day. My mother had to come down to the school to help bail me out of trouble.

In what would be a lifelong fascination for me, an attraction for women showed itself early on: at the tender age of five or six, I remember crawling under a teacher's desk to look up her dress! Though I wouldn't be sneaking under desks as I became older, seeking out women would continue for many years to come!

At home, the ongoing competition with my older brothers put me on course for my career. My father taught them the guitar, so, of course, I wanted to learn. Dad worked with me, but it was a struggle since the size of the guitar and its neck was a bit much for my young boy's hands. Rather than telling me to wait a few more years until I grew, Dad taught me how to play the ukulele. That inauspicious ukulele started my lifelong involvement with music. To this day, I'm not sure if it was a pure musical fascination or the ongoing competitiveness with my brothers that spurred me on.

Despite the size of my brothers' guitars, I would still pick them up and apply my ukulele knowledge to them.

I began some formal music education in third grade when I took up the clarinet and played it in the school band. It was my father's favorite instrument, and one of my brothers also played. Soon, I became the best clarinetist in my school's little band. By the time I reached sixth grade, I was first chair in clarinet and received the school's honor for being the best musician in the orchestra. I worked hard and made sure that I diligently practiced for at least 30 minutes a day as I was supposed to do. I did manage to take that dedication about practicing with me all through life. When I moved onto junior high, I finally ran into some real competition from older schoolmates. When a girl received first chair for clarinet, I switched over to the saxophone. That experiment didn't work so well, and I eventually dropped out of the school band.

That didn't mean I abandoned music, though; I continued to study the guitar. Some of my friends and older schoolmates played guitar, and they had a group that played its version of a country-rock-pop style. Their music was close to what The Lovin' Spoonful would play. One of the band members lived near me and had a brother my age. We went back and forth between each other's houses, learning how to play the guitar better. In the '60s, when I was in seventh grade, I got the first guitar I ever owned. It was a basic Tesco-style Japanese electric guitar with an amplifier. It was great to learn how to play this instrument, and I was constantly practicing. Some of the people I listened to on the radio were the Beach Boys and Dion. Soon, Simon and Garfunkel would also influence me. I mainly concentrated on a folksy pop-rock style of music.

The sixties also brought the dawn of the British invasion. I got into anything British, such as the movies like Alfie. I was fascinated with Peter Sellers and with the James Bond movies. Then, of course, there was the music. The British sound exploded with groups like the Beatles and the Rolling Stones. Kids all over watched these long-haired musicians on their black-and-white television sets while British bands changed the face of music.

Music on television in our household was more than just the new wave bands. My parents enjoyed almost any musical show. Sing Along with Mitch was very popular in our home, as was any show that had a celebrity singing. Johnny Mathis was a favorite of my mom, and Johnny Cash was a major influence on me. Also, my parents would go to movie musicals and buy the recordings from them to play at home. I grew up immersed in music.

When I was still a young teen, my school had a little musical get-together at lunchtime in the basement activity room. Many of the boys and girls would go down, and we'd dance to the music of the day. We were almost at the midpoint of the 1960s, and music captured the imagination of my friends and me through radio, records, and television. Many kids were putting bands together, so I thought I would join in on the fun. A neighborhood friend, Bill Johnson, played guitar, bass, piano and had some equipment. I showed up with a bigger amplifier and started playing with him. We began working out songs, and music became a more significant part of my life. I still found time, however, to do other things.

I don't think my teen years were much different from anybody else's. Having watched my older brothers getting into trouble for years, I learned to avoid suffering their consequences. I still caused lots of trouble, but I was clever enough not to get into any difficulty because of it!

I worked at a small lawn service job for some neighbors. It gave me a little income that I always ended up spending on music. Though I did my part in raising hell like any teenager, our family went to a Lutheran church every Sunday. There, I would deal with the guilt and repentance.

In high school, I wrestled and was good at hockey. During this time, the Vietnam War was raging. One of my brothers avoided the draft by joining the Marines and our family was very concerned for his safety. I have to say that I didn't feel any anti-war sentiment. I was a kid, school came easy to me, and I figured with my good grades that I could go to the Air Force Academy in Colorado for college. My dad had been a pilot, and we had an airplane without wings in our backyard. I had flown with my father a few times, which is partly what made me think that's what I wanted to do after high school. I figured that once my stint with the Air Force was over, I could become a commercial airline pilot. Back then, pilots were making $100,000 a year, a considerable amount in the '60s.

While growing up, I also spent a lot of time in the woods and the countryside. Every year, my father would take my two brothers and me up to Voyageurs National Park, near the boundary of Minnesota and Canada. The park isn't far from International Falls, Minnesota, and is a wilderness area covered with large lakes. We would fill a 14-foot aluminum boat with supplies to sustain ourselves for two weeks of living in the outdoors. Roaming in the wilderness and fishing on the lakes every year had a huge influence on me. I realized later that these experiences helped me develop the ability to survive in unfamiliar areas—a skill that came in handy with all the travel that awaited in my future. It was also here that I began my lifelong love affair with fishing. To this day, I love spending time on large bodies of water with a fishing pole in my hand.

Another influence in my mid-teens was a place in Minneapolis called Dania Hall. It was an old German community hall near the University of Minnesota. Bands were often playing psychedelic music in "the hall," and I used to hitchhike from my home all the way into Minneapolis at night. It was about a 25-mile trip one way. I used to mingle with all the "freaks," as I thought of them, and the local musicians. It was a real gathering place for the hippies, and I would enjoy a little smoking while listening to many excellent, local musicians.

These excursions certainly provided education beyond my formal schooling. I learned a little more about what people living in urban situations were facing in the sixties. I started to adjust to life in the city while living out in the suburbs. I also learned that men who picked me up while hitchhiking sometimes wanted to have a little "fun." Those lessons taught me to be cautious and to avoid confrontations with those sorts of folks. It was another lesson in survival that helped me when I went out on the road later.

While I was still a teen, my brother came home with a big, old Fender bass that he played with his friends in a little group. They were making a lot of Beach Boys-like music. That sound didn't appeal to me so much anymore; it seemed foreign. It was a little too smooth, and the songs were about warm weather, surfing, and California beaches. Living in the cold plains of Minnesota, I really couldn't relate.

I had friends who needed a bass player, so I hitchhiked two miles into Wayzata to play some music with them. I have to tell you that a Fender jazz bass in a hard-shell case weighs too much for a 96-pound boy to carry for two miles! The members of the band were my age except for the leader, Pete. He was a Scandinavian boy, kind of a long-haired rebel. He was an excellent guitarist, liked to sing, and was just a talented musician. We were playing music that included psychedelic rock with influences like Hendrix and The Doors.

Pete would gather the band at his house after school. It was a very relaxed and open place for us to get together. Pete's mom was divorced and was always working during the day. She would come home in the evening for dinner and then go back out again until late at night. She never seemed to mind what we were doing when she wasn't there. The band and I had the entire house to ourselves. At this point, my friends and I started to get into drugs and alcohol since there was no adult supervision. Girlfriends came over, and aside from playing music, there was lots of fooling around.

Our band became known for our rowdy behavior. Pete's house was the center of drinking, getting high, and rock and roll. Such a cliché, but it was a lot of fun. We became the outcasts of the town and started traveling to other places to play. We soon discovered that these travels provided opportunities to meet more young women. It was all exciting but could lead to trouble since turf battles could crop up and local guys didn't want their girls to hang with the out-of-town riffraff. Definite territorial boundaries existed in those days in Minnesota. It seemed like one of us in the band was always getting beat up by somebody, or we were getting chased out of town by a carload of teens. If nothing else, these experiences added excitement and color to growing up! I vividly remember one car chase when we were in my friend's father's 1959 pink Cadillac. We were zipping through roads cut out of the middle of cornfields trying to get away from a bunch of redneck teens from another town.

While it certainly was not the Juilliard School of Music, I had a great time cutting my teeth on music and performing during this period. This part of my music education wasn't anything that I would recommend as a blueprint for a music career today, but it was effective. As far as I can remember, the band's name was The Greenery, a reference to pot. Much of the music we played was in the category of "psychedelic." All members of the band had a couple of songs they would sing. I did one or two, but Pete carried the load as the leader.

At around 16, I ran into a severe setback when showing off to some girls while riding a motorcycle. Attempting to do some Steve McQueen-type jumps that the actor had made famous in the film The Great Escape, I broke my leg when a jump went horribly wrong. The fracture effectively ended my hockey career, as I wore a full leg cast that kept me at home for five months. For three of those months, I missed school, so teachers would come to my house to bring my lessons. For the first time in my life, I fell behind in school. When I finally got back to the classroom, I couldn't catch up, and my grades began to suffer.

That ill-fated motorcycle stunt made such a difference in my plans for the future. School became difficult, and college—let alone the Air Force Academy—no longer seemed like a viable option. At about the same time, though, one of my band mates started focusing on the blues. Many of the songs played by some of the famous rockers of the day were blues oriented. My buddy and I would go to the library to check out blues records, and we would spend hours listening to them. My friend's father was an attorney and would be gone most of the day. We would bring our blues records into the basement and listen to them endlessly while trying to imitate the music with our guitars.

That was the start of the blues thing for me. I was seventeen and psychedelic rock was still the most popular form of music for most kids. Nevertheless, I began concentrating on the blues. I grew my hair long and periodically got kicked out of school for smoking. I started to feel persecuted and treated as an outcast. Since school wasn't going so well anyway, I didn't mind so much and began to see a new path for my life. I did manage to graduate high school in 1969, a few months after turning eighteen. I had no further interest in education, but made sure I got a diploma because I knew my mother would be proud of me for that. At this point, I knew music was my passion and what I wanted to do with my life.

At around 16, I ran into a severe setback when showing off to some girls while riding a motorcycle. Attempting to do some Steve McQueen-type jumps that the actor had made famous in the film The Great Escape, I broke my leg when a jump went horribly wrong. The fracture effectively ended my hockey career, as I wore a full leg cast that kept me at home for five months. For three of those months, I missed school, so teachers would come to my house to bring my lessons. For the first time in my life, I fell behind in school. When I finally got back to the classroom, I couldn't catch up, and my grades began to suffer.

That ill-fated motorcycle stunt made such a difference in my plans for the future. School became difficult, and college—let alone the Air Force Academy—no longer seemed like a viable option. At about the same time, though, one of my band mates started focusing on the blues. Many of the songs played by some of the famous rockers of the day were blues oriented. My buddy and I would go to the library to check out blues records, and we would spend hours listening to them. My friend's father was an attorney and would be gone most of the day. We would bring our blues records into the basement and listen to them endlessly while trying to imitate the music with our guitars.

That was the start of the blues thing for me. I was seventeen and psychedelic rock was still the most popular form of music for most kids. Nevertheless, I began concentrating on the blues. I grew my hair long and periodically got kicked out of school for smoking. I started to feel persecuted and treated as an outcast. Since school wasn't going so well anyway, I didn't mind so much and began to see a new path for my life. I did manage to graduate high school in 1969, a few months after turning eighteen. I had no further interest in education, but made sure I got a diploma because I knew my mother would be proud of me for that. At this point, I knew music was my passion and what I wanted to do with my life.

2

Early Adulthood Travels

For a while, I was playing some music with a buddy of mine named Dave Gove. Things changed when Dave's girlfriend got pregnant and they decided to marry. To pull this marriage off, I helped him break into his father's law office and stole a form allowing underage marriage. We filled it out, signed his father's name to it, and then forged her mother's signature. Equipped with the proper documents, we drove 300 miles to South Dakota to get them married! Together, the three of us moved to the big city of Minneapolis and lived in a cheap little one-bedroom duplex in the southern part of the city. It was near Lake Street, where there were plenty of musical joints along the road. When the baby was born, I found myself part of this nurturing household. It was then that I started pursuing a musical career in earnest. The blues opened the door to my future.

I reckon you can say that I began my adult years with that move to the city. I was 18, schooling was over, and now I had to make a living. Some friends and I started a little group called the Lake Street Stink Band. It was an odd name, but the music we played was very low down and stinky if I had to describe it. While it wasn't terrific blues, it was still the blues. It wasn't all that sophisticated, but we were playing, and that's all that counted. We used to play in this place called the Joint Bar near the University of Minnesota in the West Bank area on Cedar Avenue. It was your typical bar, and a group named Willy Murphy and the Bumble Bees was playing the weekends there. The drinking age was 21, and we weren't old enough to go to the bars. Instead, we'd hang around on the outside, listening to the music coming out the doors and through the walls. One day we decided to see if they'd be willing to let us play during the week. They did! The bar hired us to play four nights a week, Monday through Thursday. We couldn't drink, but we were able to work in the bar. It was crazy times, but we got to play quite a bit in those early years. I was new to the music scene and this provided a good educational experience.

Another place that we played often was even further out of the area, in Excelsior, Minnesota. It was a beer joint called Humple Myers, and it was one of those spots out in the countryside that had a lot of people hanging out. The place always had live music going, so I started playing there, too. That was how our early days in bars went.

Around this time, I connected with a guy who was a combination guitarist, harmonica player, and singer. His name was Wayne White and we formed a duo. We started playing in a couple of places around Minneapolis. One that was quite famous was called the Triangle Bar. Spider John Koerner used to play there when he was part of the group Koerner, Ray, and Glover–they were a popular folk blues trio. I well remember standing outside, watching him through the door as he performed, and telling myself that I was going to play on that stage one day. It wasn't long after that Wayne and I did end up playing there.

At that time, I was playing some acoustic slide guitar and regular blues guitar, along with playing in the band. I was quite busy with the group and the duo. We weren't making much money, but I was really getting into this blues thing and soaking up all I could.

After having my high school academic career go south and barely managing to graduate, imagine the weirdness of finding myself at 18, having a music class at the University of Minnesota invite Wayne and me to lecture! I was absolutely flattered and was proud to be a guest lecturer at the college level. I didn't really know much about blues at the time, but I knew more than almost everyone else around the area. It was a defining moment for me. I realized that the blues was a valuable music form and that it was something I wanted to continue to be a part of and to support.

When I was around 19, I went to the Ann Arbor Blues Festival. While there, I was invited to play in a band in Delaware, Ohio. I had a friend named Bob Bingham who attended Ohio Wesleyan University. It was an upscale university and Bob was in a band with other college frat boys. They needed a guitar player and gave me a call. I traveled by Greyhound from Minnesota to Ohio to get together with these boys. We practiced and partied at their fraternity house. When I think back to that time, I can't help but think of the movie Animal House with John Belushi. When I saw that movie, years later, it reminded me so much of my time at that frat house in Ohio. Given the parallels, you would think they used Wesleyan as a model for the movie.

Playing with the band in Ohio was quite a musical journey for me. We were certainly successful in the area, but I knew what was waiting for me back home and was anxious to be there. I only lasted through the winter, spring, and autumn.

When I moved back home to Minnesota, I was kind of on my own, though Wayne and I still did some playing together.

Around 1970, when I was still 19, I hitchhiked with Wayne to Stevens Point, Wisconsin, for a big rock festival. It was a three-day fest and was an exciting experience for us. From there, we hitchhiked up to Canada and tried to cross over to see what the music scene was like there. We thought that after doing that, we'd work our way back down through New York. However, we never got to visit our neighbor to the north. When we got to the border, the Canadian authorities made us turn around. The Vietnam War was going hot and heavy, and we were draft age and were in the lottery to go into military service. Canadian border guards were very suspicious of guys my age trying to cross into Canada.

When the Canadian authorities turned us back, it was probably the best thing that ever happened because we worked our way down to Ann Arbor. We rambled into the city and started looking for places to play. We ended up at a coffee house called The Arc, and then got invited to play at a place called Mr. Flood's Party. They liked us so much that they gave us free beer on the first night, beer and wine on the second night, and all the liquor we could drink on the third. It was wild! I imagine the music suffered from all the booze we drank, but it was party time. When you play in bars, you learn to party and get people excited so they share the moment.

My early music training took me into some strange situations. There was one night when we were playing the bars and had nowhere to stay. As we ambled down to the railroad tracks, I remember hearing the melody for one of the songs that I would write in one of my early grooves. Finding a place to sleep was always an adventure. One night, we met up with some hippies and crashed at their house. They told us that the great Muddy Waters was performing in Detroit.

So, we hopped on a Greyhound and made it to the show. Wow! Muddy Waters was terrific and everything I thought he would be.

From Detroit, we hitchhiked back to Minnesota. I can't recall the exact way everything went down, but it definitely taught me about the importance of timing. I think that partly because we were playing blues in the bars there, the music caught on. The bar owners in the area got in touch with the old blues guys and started bringing them into town. When we got back to town, a lot of old blues guys were coming too Minneapolis to perform. At about the same time, the University of Minnesota found some way to connect with the veteran blues guys from the South and brought them in to do shows on campus. It helped to be in the right place at the right time.

We had acoustic players flowing into the city and a flood of Mississippi bluesmen coming up from the South from cities like Memphis. Soon enough, the Chicago blues also started coming into town. There was a constant flow of bluesmen and women; it was just fabulous! I remember going through a seminar with Mississippi Fred McDowell at the university and then seeing him perform later that night for the students. During that concert, Mississippi Fred was on stage with a line of drinks in front of him and a front row of college girls in the audience. That's when I decided that I wanted to be an acoustic blues musician!

Right about then—and I mean, literally, during the concert—Wayne and I got the word that we were wanted back in Ann Arbor because Mr. Flood's Party needed to book us to perform for three nights. We rushed out of the concert, got on a bus and rode through the night, but we didn't quite make it. We were a couple of hours late, so we played for free for the abbreviated first night, but then we did two more nights for some reasonable pay. It was flattering and encouraging to realize that if you get out there and make positive connections, then good things might come back to you.

Meanwhile, back in Minnesota, the drinking age went from age 21 to 18. Just like that, you had all these young people flooding the bars. It was strange to all of a sudden see teenagers piled into the bars where we were playing blues. As I said earlier, we had all these old blues guys in town, and everybody in Minneapolis was getting hooked on this music. The bars swelled every single night with hordes that were there for the blues. These crowds got to hear the most authentic blues performers and it was just a magical time.

My good friend Wayne White was singing with us in the Lake Street Stink Band. We were also still performing together in the duo and in another trio we had. I was playing a whole lot of bass guitar and six-string guitar with a Martin D-18. I'd been looking around for a National steel-body slide guitar for a while at this point. Bukka White happened to play one of these guitars and after Wayne and I had the good fortune to open a couple shows for him, I was more convinced than ever that I had to have one.

After Wayne moved to Texas and fell in love with Willie Nelson's music, I became aware that some Minnesota guys that I had connections with had bought a bar in Winter Park, Colorado. I headed out that way with the remainder of the Lake Street Stink Bank and we started playing gigs. While in Colorado, I hooked up with my old buddy from Wesleyan University, Bob Bingham. Bob was a bit of a rebel and a band hopper. He'd recently rambled through California playing gigs and had met a few blues guys over there. One of these guys was Kim Wilson, who'd eventually go on to quite a bit of fame and glory with The Fabulous Thunderbirds. Bob and Kim had been playing in a band together and the next thing I knew, they'd contacted me and asked if I could play bass. I said, "Sure, why not!"

We went back to Minneapolis and the band was called Aces, Straights, and Shuffles. Kim Wilson was the leader, playing harmonica and singing. We played all around the Midwest from 1972–1974. We got to hang out with a lot of the great, old blues artists and played with them when they came through. We backed some of them up, and luckily, Willie Dixon heard a recording of our band and helped us to get a recording contract.

When you are young, you think that getting such a contract will put you on the road to success. For the majority of musical artists, however, that isn't the case. We did head into the studio, cut a few tracks, and even released a single. But the album got scrapped for some reason. This, combined with the slight tensions that had arisen between certain members of the band, marked the end to Aces, Straights, and Shuffles. Kim had heard about the burgeoning blues scene down in Austin, Texas. Soon enough, he moved down there and started The Fabulous Thunderbirds with Jimmie Vaughan.

Sometime around 1975 or so, I too traveled to Austin with some buddies. We put together a band called Crossroads and started playing the blues around all the local joints. Wayne White was also down there, so he and I were able to pick up our duo act again. It was a great time, but after a while I headed back up north to resume my life in Minnesota.

3

The Northwoods and First Solo Gigs

There's a later chapter where I'll talk more extensively about my ex-wives, but I met the first of four in 1977. Greta was a beautiful Scandinavian girl and incredible dancer who caught my eye in the audience one night. I was 26 years old at the time and we got to know each other for a little while before marrying in June.

Greta and I spent some time traveling through Mexico and we had some really crazy times down there. Despite our poverty, we made the best of it and took little trips all over. We went by train to the islands off the coast of Yucatan Mujeres and back. I think the round trip back then was all of 15 dollars in second class. I played a little music in some of the bars and cantinas along the way, trying to see if there was a possibility of a solo career for old Kent DuChaine. I did a little bit of singing and a lot of playing in exotic, faraway places. That trip took a few weeks. When we were coming back, we visited a lot of the Mayan ruins and spent some time in Mexico City. Eventually, we made our way back up to Texas and then back home to Minnesota.

Around that time, my brother Greg bought a resort up in the Northwoods of Minnesota. He wanted to open up a campground on Big Sandy Lake in conjunction with the resort. He asked if my wife and I would be interested in coming up there to live, develop the campground and manage it. I did that for three years. Greg was always looking for inexpensive labor, so I invited Wayne White to come up to work. He helped me cut campgrounds out of the raw wilderness along the lakeside. Once Wayne was with me, we still had musical opportunities. We did a lot of work for KAXE, a public radio station in northern Minnesota, out of Grand Rapids. We had some opportunities to play on the radio and for fundraising events. We also did some little festival shows and met a lot of the Northwoods musicians. One radio announcer and his gal had a big party every year called the Deer Lake Boogie, and they invited Wayne and me to come and play at that. It was a weekend of music and more music at the very top of Minnesota near the Canadian border. We had good times at the Deer Lake Boogie.

We also did these Jack Pine Jamborees, special radio programs that the station aired live. All in all, we made great connections over the three years that we worked there.

When winter hit in the northland where we were living, everything shut down. We're talking very snowy, arctic weather up there in the wilderness. With not much to do, my wife and I decided to travel south to see what we could find.

This trip south was more extensive than the first time I rambled around that area. We traveled through Mexico and into Central America this time around. It was a smart idea to skip the countries having revolutions, so we avoided places like El Salvador. However, we did fly into Managua in

Nicaragua just as the Sandinistas were bombing the capital. That was a little too exciting, so we didn't stay long. We didn't make it as far as Panama, but we did visit Costa Rica. Guatemala was fabulous, and, of course, we explored new places in Mexico. All in all, it was an excellent way to spend the winter.

It was around this time that I had a falling out with my brother, Greg. I had bought a house on one of his properties where he had several rental homes. He talked me into purchasing the house and it was great for a while. The resort campground I was managing was going well, but I started backing off when I had the issue with my brother. No matter, though, since there was plenty of work around the area. When Greta and I settled into our new house, I went out looking for cook work again. I found good jobs working for old chef friends in country clubs.

I got a job at Ichiban, a Japanese steakhouse, and became the head chef there. It was a very busy time of working, working, and more working. There seemed to be very little time for anything else but working, paying bills, and trying to keep things happy and healthy at home. This was probably the longest I went without playing a lot of music, though Wayne White and I did connect with my cousin Barry Johnson who was playing the bass. We had a little trio and played all around the area when there was free time, so that was good.

I was pretty much working six days a week for about 14 hours each day and busting it. I was making lots of money, and that was great, but there was no time for anything else. Whenever I had a day off, I might go off and do a little fishing. I guess I should have spent some of that time with the first ex-wife, but that's life!

Eventually, I got tired of always working and decided I was going to become a fishing guide and an outdoor sports journalist. I figured I'd write articles for fishing and hunting magazines since I'd spent a lot of time out in the woods and on the water and knew my way around lakes, rivers, and trails. Plus, I was fairly good at capturing the prey, so to speak.

My new plans would also dovetail nicely with my love of taking pictures. This helped to crystallize my thinking–so I planned to write articles and provide the accompanying photos for sporting magazines, and also become a fishing guide. I did all the research about writing and how much money I could make. I printed up guide brochures and offered my services. I put them around in local hotels and immediately started to get calls. It was fabulous!

Here I was, starting this new career as a fishing guide, and all of a sudden, my brother came back to me. He said, "Kent, I want you to come up and do some cooking in my restaurant at the resort." I figured I could run up there and cook, then do some fishing, guiding, and writing articles during the week, and then come home on the weekends and spend time with Greta. She had enrolled at the university and couldn't come with me for the week. It worked out great for me, but not for her. She decided that she wanted to break up the relationship, which was okay with me. I borrowed a bunch of money from my brother to pay for her half of the house, and the marriage to Greta was over.

So in 1981 or '82, I was living in the Northwoods working as a chef for my brother for six or seven days a week. I was also playing as an outdoor guide in what spare time I had and trying to get my solo career going. My first solo show was up north because I didn't want to play in front of anyone I knew. For all the performing I had done up to that point, I was frightened to death of being out there on my own. I think the first place I played at was at a little bar called the Sand Point. It was a dance hall on the same lake where my brother had his resort and campground. It was my first solo show where I set up, performed, and got paid. I remember being terrified about getting on stage, but the audience applauded and enjoyed it. Their response was encouraging, and I figured maybe I really could stand up there to sing and play by myself. It doesn't take much to raise my confidence level a little bit, so I decided I would venture to the big city of Minneapolis and try to book some solo shows down there.

    I went and booked a show at a place called the Artist Quarter, where Wayne and I had played as a duo. Wouldn't you know that all my friends and all my band mates from the past showed up. Oh, man, I was frightened! It was the most excruciating gig I've ever done. I told myself I just needed to get through the first song and then I'd be okay. If it didn't get a favorable reaction, I'd bail out and get the hell out of there. To my great surprise, everyone applauded! So, I thought, "Oh, I'll do another song and see how that goes." I carried on and got through the first set. At the break, all my friends were very supportive. I knew it was crap, but I was bound and determined to make this work.

    That is how my solo career started. I did some playing on the radio up north and, soon, was becoming a little bit of a Northwoods blues star. I was also playing in my home area of Minneapolis, where the blues was extremely popular.

    I put a ton of miles on my car. When I finished up at the resort on Sunday, I'd drive back to Minneapolis in time for the last call on Sunday night. I would look for cool spots to go to and try to get a gig to play on Monday, which was my day off from the resort. Then it was back north again to be at work on Tuesday. Sunday was my only off night each week, and it was working out fine. I was running across potential future ex-wives and having fun. I still had the house in town where I could duck in for sleep. It was a duplex, so I rented out both units and set up a little homey spot for myself in the basement. My weeks were crazy, but there was a peculiar, mad structure to my schedule. It was good to have a place to call home whether I was up in the woods or back in town.

By March, things had really gotten slower. My brother had closed his place for the winter and it hadn't opened back up yet. There was a place in Minneapolis that I had started playing called the Viking Bar. It was a Bohemian spot on the West Bank of the University of Minnesota. All the bars were within an easy walk of each other. One night I was hanging out in the Viking Bar with a few friends. I remember saying, "Hey, it's Mardi Gras. Let's go down to New Orleans!"

We piled into the blue van I was driving at the time and drove 1,200 miles to New Orleans to party at Mardi Gras. I played a little on the streets and got some time playing in a couple of bars. It was all one big party and was incredible. If you ever get invited down to Mardi Gras, go! It will be a time you'll remember for the rest of your life. That plug is only my opinion and was not paid for by the city of New Orleans.

I returned north in one piece, more or less, and it was back to the routine of cooking at the resort, fishing, and traveling back to Minneapolis once a week to play in a bar. It was a great time. On occasion, I'd play at the club in the resort when I finished my cooking chores. I had friends from the city coming up to relax and play music, and we'd have a lot of fun.

At some point in that time, I ran into a childhood friend of mine named Tommy Burns. He played harmonica, and we had played together when we traveled to Winter Park, Colorado. At this time, Tommy was playing harmonica with Lazy Bill Lucas, who we thought of as the "Godfather of the Blues." Lucas was an old, blind, Black pianist who played excellent blues. He had a massive influence on my development as a blues player. Bill and Tommy were playing in a lot of the same clubs as I was, so I'd sometimes go and hang out with them when I was in town on the weekends. One night, I was watching them perform and Bill wasn't feeling well. I told Bill, "I'll step in and finish the show for you. Just sit down and relax." Tragically, he died from a heart attack later that night.

Tommy was now out of work, so I offered to play some gigs with him. He was a good friend and a great harmonica player, so we started playing together regularly. During this time, though, Tommy was getting into trouble with his ex in Minneapolis. He'd had to leave town because of an altercation with his ex's new boyfriend. Since the law was looking for Tommy, I said, "Well, come with me, and we'll hide you out." So, we did that up in the Northwoods. He worked for my brother for about three months. It was kind of Greg to have given Tommy a job.

Tommy and I decided that when winter came, we were going back to Colorado. The plan was to go out there for a week in early October, run around the mountains and book gigs for the winter. Then we'd come back and work for my brother some more. We'd make some good money beating out the wild rice. Yup, I did say wild rice. You might not know this, but Minnesota has more acres of wild rice than any other state in the country. It must be all our lakes. We spent the better part of three weeks beating those rice canes and collecting wild rice to make enough money so that we could make this winter tour of Colorado happen. If you could make $100 a day beating wild rice, you were doing great. We didn't quite make that much every day but did well enough to have a substantial bundle when Tommy and I headed to Colorado.

4

Skin and Bones Take Colorado and New Orleans

Now I've had quite a few vehicles through the years, and in 1982 I was driving a 1956 Cadillac limousine that I'd named "Marilyn," which Tommy and I took to Colorado. I vividly remember driving north along the Front Range out of Winter Park, and heading up to Steamboat Springs. We wanted to get up there and see if there were some places we could play. It was the middle of a beautiful and clear night with a full moon, and Tommy had passed out. We were driving into an area they call the Summit, just south of Steamboat Springs. It was about a 20 mile flat run on top of the world!

I remember turning off my car lights and driving that 20 miles in the dark. That stunt might have been pretty crazy, but the moon was shining so brightly that the snow was glistening and lighting everything up. It wasn't the first or last time that I'd done a crazy thing like that and the opportunity was too special a moment to pass up.

We still had a lot of old school friends in Colorado, including the ones that owned the Dew Drop Inn, which was the mountain ski resort lodge where we performed. The inn gave us a home base. We played many gigs up and down the Front Range of the Rockies in ski resorts and all kinds of bars.

Now Marilyn stuck out like a sore thumb in Colorado, with the Minnesota plates and a couple of scruffy looking jokers tooling around inside. We were pulled over and harassed by the cops often, but never actually arrested for anything. Finally, one night in February, the Fort Collins Police pulled us over and told us that if we didn't get the hell out of town, they'd find something to bust us for. This was all right with us because it was Mardi Gras time again and we were planning to head to New Orleans anyway. Getting kicked out of town just hastened our journey.

We blew through Colorado, New Mexico, and Texas into Louisiana. When we hit New Orleans, I had 15 cents in my pocket. Tommy had enough for a 6-pack of beer, so he was all set. We started hitting the French Quarter, pitching our duo, Skin and Bones; Tommy was "Skin" and I was "Bones." We'd go into bars and ask if we could come in and play a little. Maybe it would be an audition for a future gig, or we'd play a little bit and pass the hat to see if we could get a drink or two as the old bluesmen would do.

When we started trying to get gigs, we either were thrown out or turned down in the first three spots we hit. At the fourth place called Lord VJ's–which was down on the edge of the Quarter–the manager said, "Come on in and play. If we like you, we'll buy you a drink." Well, that deal really worked; we passed the hat and it was full of money when it got back to us! Somebody offered us a place to stay and things started looking better. We were told to go park in the parking lot of an apartment building that was near the area. That way, we'd be off the street, and we could come in the next day and use the people's apartment to get cleaned up and chill out a little bit.

We were so excited by all this good fortune that we played until three or four o'clock in the morning. We partied with everybody and then took off from Lord VJ's, heading to the place where we were going to park. We were right in the middle of New Orleans on Canal Street when the drive shaft fell out of Marilyn! What a drag! We were broke down and drunk in the center of NOLA. We had a little bit of money from passing the hat, so we called a tow truck. We wired the driveshaft back into Marilyn, and got towed to our destination. We slept in the car there until morning.

Waking up was a bit of a mind-blowing experience. I was in the back seat, and the windows were tinted all the way around the car except for the front windshield. Nobody could really see in the Cadillac. Tommy was stretched out in the front seat asleep. When I looked out my window into the parking lot, there were ten police officials out there! It looked like an assortment of state troopers, some federal types, and the locals, complete with paddy wagons. I watched and wondered what the heck was going on. Then I saw that the cops were leading a line of handcuffed people out of this apartment building.

I was, of course, a little bit freaked out now because we were right in the middle of this situation. I watched as the cops carried out bags that looked like they might hold dope. They had guns out, and these little pencil wands that they were using to parade people down to the paddy wagons. All of a sudden, Tommy stirred and started kicking at the door because he was a little too tall to be completely stretched out in the limo. I told him, "Tommy, please be quiet. There's a big drug bust going on all around us." Finally, fully awake, he looked out; sure enough, it was all going down just as I'd told him.

We kept watching what was going on through the tinted windows. The paddy wagons finally drove off, and all the cops were standing around, slapping each other on the back for a job well done. I saw one big, tall blond-headed state trooper look over at the Cadillac. He started walking our way with his hand on his gun. He walked right up to the Cadillac, so I immediately opened the door. I got out, put my hands on the outside of the car and assumed the position. Tommy started to crawl out, too. I immediately started talking to the officer and told him that I'd been watching everything that went down. I told him that we had been invited to this place to park so that we were off the street and could go in and use the facilities to get cleaned up.

By then, all the other cops started moving toward us, and the next thing we knew, they were shaking us down. I told them that we were musicians and had money in our pockets; we were not bums. As I was trying to explain all this to them, they told me to shut up. Tommy started moving around, and the cops said to him that if he didn't put his hands back on the car, they were going to rip his arms off and beat him with them. You don't mess with the New Orleans cops!

The cops then started searching us. We didn't have anything much, but I was a little concerned because we did have some psychedelics tucked underneath the panel and pushed behind the radio. They began going through the limo, looking underneath the dashboard and the seats. They dug through the glove box. As I watched them, I talked and talked, trying to distract them as they reached up there and felt around. Fortunately, they didn't find anything.

After that search, they tore the front seat out. I mean they literally ripped it out of its bindings and dragged it out into the parking lot. They were looking all over on the floor, and I started to get a little nervous. When we had left Minnesota, we had had a big bag of smoke with us. It was to be our stash for the trip. In the middle of the night, stoned out of our brains, we had started throwing all our trash out. I thought that we'd thrown that smoke out along with our debris because we had become very paranoid. We had dozens of beer cans in the car, and we unloaded it all on the road. It was a horrible thing to do on a couple of levels, but we didn't want to have an altercation with the law. I assumed that we had thrown all the pot out because we couldn't find it. Now the cops were tearing the car apart, and I was very worried that they were going to find this huge bag. It was Minnesota Green, and it was terrible quality, but it could still land us in jail. I finally gave out a breath of relief when they didn't find a thing. It looked like the situation was getting better for us, and then the cops asked me if I had any dangerous weapons. I said, "Yes!"

The cops immediately perked up. "Where?" one asked.

I said, "Well, there's a knife in the visor over the driver's seat. It's a special knife that I bought in Guatemala. It's handmade with a bone handle, and it's a kind of a ceremonial knife."

They grabbed the knife out of the car and looked it over to see if it had any blood on it. There was nothing illegal about my having the knife, so now they were getting frustrated. Next, they went to the back of the car to check the trunk. It was enormous and jammed full of tires and musical equipment. They were digging through everything, trying to find anything that they could pin on us. They opened Tommy's laundry bag; he hadn't done his laundry since we'd left Minnesota. After opening that bag, they stepped back a couple of steps because of the smell. It reeked! That was the end of the search. They pushed Tommy's laundry bag back in the trunk and closed it up. One of the cops said to us, "You boys are free to go, but don't let us catch you on the streets of New Orleans, or we're dragging you down to central lockup. You don't wanna go to central lockup during Mardi Gras."

After all the excitement, we didn't want to go into the building to clean up because we still didn't know what was going on there with all the arrests that were made. We were stuck. The Caddy was busted up, and we couldn't just drive away. We walked back into the French Quarter and went to Lord VJ's. The owner was a cool cat who had a limo service that he used to pick up people from different bars and bring them back to his bar. He also used it if his patrons wanted to go to another bar. He'd have someone drive us in his big, white limo whose driver did quite well with tips. The owner loaned us some money in advance of our playing his place every night. We arranged to have the Caddy towed to a shop to fix the driveshaft. The mechanic there took a day or two, but he installed some new ball joints into the drive shaft of Marilyn, and we were soon back on the road, ready to roll.

Lord VJ's owner wanted us to play every night from 9 until midnight, 14 nights in a row. Since we were set there, we went looking for other places to play. One of them, Miss Molly's, was a little gay bar. We now had credibility because of playing at Lord VJ's, and we were told we could play there every night if we wanted. We were booked there from 1 a.m. to 4:00 a.m.

There was another place called Maxwell's, which was on Maxwell Street right off Bourbon Street. It booked us for the late-late set so we'd go there about 4 a.m. and play till about 8 a.m. The owner of that place happened to have a parking lot a block down Maxwell Street. He said, "You boys can park your Caddy there, and it'll be safe. I'll pay for it and take it out of your pay."

So, for two weeks, we played three clubs a night, starting about 9 at night and finishing 8 the next morning. We had

Marilyn there a block off Bourbon Street where we could crash when done playing. It was perfect, absolutely perfect! We partied hard for 14 nights at Mardi Gras. We'd play all night long for 12 hours and start our heavy drinking. It was an incredibly fun two weeks.

Interestingly, parked next to Marilyn was a big, old bus for New Orleans' central lockup. Cops were always hauling people into that big bus. They'd fill it up and take the culprits away. Then, the cops would bring the bus back, park it, and fill it up again. There was always a parade of people getting arrested all during Mardi Gras. However, we were safe and continued to party and have a wonderful time!

You never knew what would happen during Mardi Gras. One night I was on a corner of Bourbon, and there was this big club with a second-floor deck and a group of gay boys were partying like wild men. In front of the club were a bunch of fundamentalist Christians with signs telling the gay boys they were going to hell. It wasn't a silent protest either. They were yelling and screaming their heads off at the gays. On the other corner were a bunch of bikers that were cursing and swearing at the Christians. On the third corner were the cops, watching it all go down. It was a pretty dramatic scene. Nothing ever got quite out of hand, but it was definitely worth remembering!

There's always a big parade on Fat Tuesday when Mardi Gras ends. I remember locking arms with Tommy during the parade, which started on Canal Street. The crowd started growing quickly and began charging down the street like cattle being pushed into a pen. Tommy and I dug our feet into the pavement to keep from getting overrun by the crowd. People panicked and climbed the light poles along the street so they didn't get run over. We partied hard! In addition to almost being stomped to death in a parade, Lulu, the red-headed Cajun Queen, gave me a case of the clap. Then at midnight on Fat Tuesday, the cops came in and closed the city down. The next morning, the streets were absolutely quiet.

Mardi Gras was over, so Tommy and I packed into Marilyn and headed east toward the beaches and sunshine of Florida.

5

Ramblin' Around the Gulf Coast and the Keys

We followed the Gulf Coast and Marilyn cruised into the Florida Panhandle just in time for spring break; there were half-naked co-eds everywhere on the beautiful, white sand beaches. The first place we worked was on the coast between Alabama and Florida. Literally! The stateline runs right through the middle of the bar, so it's called the Flora-Bama. Joe Gilchrist was the owner, and he took Tommy and me under his wing, gave us some gigs and set us up interviews with the local newspapers. After that, Skin and Bones played the Flora-Bama quite often. In latter years, the joint has become internationaly know as a great music venue and gained additional fame when featured in John Grisham's best-selling novel, The Firm.

Tommy and I started working all over the beaches of the Gulf Coast. This was my first big experience with living in a different climate in the wintertime, and it was a lot nicer basking in the sun instead of dealing with sub-zero temperatures. Many of the musicians we ran into invited us to a bunch of cool spots, so we covered the Florida coast from Navarre to Pensacola, Fort Walton Beach and Destin. Fort Walton Beach and Destin were, and still are, wonderful places to enjoy spring break. People were partying everywhere. I guess that's when I met this crazy redhead from Alabama who was working at the Flora-Bama. Her name was Lisa and she was the boss' girlfriend, but she fancied me, and eventually, we hooked up.

In Pensacola, we managed to land a great gig at a bar called Trader John's. Trader John was an old navy pilot who, when he retired, started the bar and filled it up with memorabilia from the U.S. Navy. He had a big navy airplane hanging from the ceiling. His place was unique as all the chairs around the bar were like the ones you found in a dental office. Many famous people frequented Trader John's. These included some who were soon to be presidents, senators, prominent businessmen, and future movie personalities. Writers like Capote and Hemmingway, when they were alive, frequented Trader John's because of its unique atmosphere. Trader John also owned a strip club next door, and the manager was quite the old guy, but very cool. While many often think musicians are a colorful lot, the owners of the places they play can often be characters as well.

Soon it was time to head home and, thankfully, Marilyn was running well enough to get us back up north. This was the early '80s, and I was still working for my brother in the summer at the resort up in Minnesota. It was the same routine of cooking, fishing, playing some local places, and running to Minneapolis one day a week for a gig. In between my duties at the resort, Tommy and I had Skin and Bones doing really well, and Marilyn faithfully transported us back and forth to Minneapolis and throughout the Midwest at different times.

Over in St. Paul, a new place called Wilebski's Blues Saloon had opened. Ted Wilebski would bring up blues artists from Chicago to play the place. Tommy and I were available as an opening act, so we started a lot of shows for Ted. Many of the performers were second-tier blues guys, but some of them were top dogs like Buddy Guy and cats like that. Old Ted looked out for us because he appreciated what we were doing for him. We were playing some authentic, old-style blues.

When autumn came, it was time to close down the resort, and that's when Tommy and I decided we were going to make the run down to Key West. Spending winter in warm weather rather than freezing our asses off in Minnesota was increasingly appealing to us. On the way, though, we headed back to the Gulf Coast and played some at the Flora-Bama. When we made this run, we'd usually grab a couple of cases of beer and hit the road. Totally illegal, but that's how we did it. At the Flora-Bama, I reconnected with Lisa, the redhead who eventually became the second ex-wife.

Lisa was quite wild and she came from a bit of money; her parents had a big plantation-style home on the banks of a bay on the Gulf Coast. I managed to talk her into coming to Key West with Tommy and me, so we did some psychedelics and took off.

She had no qualms about giving me pleasure as we were driving with Tommy sitting next to us. It was odd, but that's the way she was. We ended up kicking around Key West in Marilyn and hiding out at the airport to sleep in the Caddy. It was a constant game of hide-n-seek with the cops when it came to finding spots to sleep. Tommy didn't like sleeping in the limo with us, so he slept outside. One morning, he came to the car and said kids who were waiting for a bus were throwing rocks at him. It woke him up when the rocks started landing near him. These kids were hollering, "Let's throw rocks at the bum in the bushes!" Tommy didn't take too kindly to being called a "bum in the bushes," so we found those little boys at a local store. We gave them a talking to about what would happen if they didn't stop. They stopped.

Key West was great fun. We found this really cool late night spot called The Green Parrot, and we played at Captain Tony's and Rick's on many other nights. Tommy and I would introduce ourselves at these places and offer to play for free beer and letting us pass the hat. The next thing we knew, we had gigs all over Key West. We played just about every night of the week somewhere. We also played at the famous Sloppy Joe's, which was one of Hemmingway's old haunts. Captain Tony's bar was the original Sloppy Joe's. Captain Tony had all kinds of deals going on in KeyWest. He sold the rights to the Sloppy Joe's name, and the owners moved the establishment up to the corner.

Captain Tony was an old character who was from the Jersey area and ran numbers for the mob. Apparently, he was getting information on the winners of horse races before they were broadcast and placing his bets at the last second. The mob got hip to him, took him out and beat him to a pulp. They left him for dead in some junkyard in New Jersey. Captain Tony said he hightailed it out of there heading as far as he could, and ending up in Key West. He sold guns to Castro and also sold them to the Bay of Pigs' soldiers who were trying to take back Cuba. He was an equal opportunity mobster and a real character. You had to love this old guy!

So, we had all these gigs, and Lisa was still with us. Then Tommy and I had a falling out and ended up breaking up. Tommy was homesick, so he jumped on a Greyhound bus and went back to Minnesota. He eventually started working in Chicago as a harmonica player for a big, Black gal named Queen Sylvia, who played the bass.

Anyway, I stayed on in Key West with my redheaded Cajun Queen. We lived out of Marilyn until April came around and it was time to work our way back north. It was around this time that I stopped working for my brother up north, but I still made the annual trip to Minnesota. Lisa came along, and I played at some of my old bars around Minneapolis. Soon we headed back to Florida, where I mainly kicked around the Gulf Coast and the Keys.

I think it was in 1984 that I was back in Key West and made my first solo recording. Audience members would ask for a recording from time to time, so I finally bought a tape deck cassette recorder. I'd take it to shows and put together a live recording at Captain Tony's. The recorder was a double cassette deck, and I spent all day running off recordings of my show. It was very low-tech!

Around that time, we met an ole long-haired hippy named Pirate Bill who lived down in the Virgin Islands. He was a dude that worked on a salvage boat for Mel Fisher, an American treasure hunter best known for finding the 1622 wreck of the Nuestra Señora de Atocha. Pirate Bill was diving on the Spanish wreck around then. He had invited us down to the Virgin Islands, and at the end of the season in Key West, we locked Marilyn up and flew down for a month.

Bill was an old-timer who knew his way around the islands. At this point, he had lived there for a long time and had a ton of connections. He got me gigs for almost every night of the week. We partied hard with Bill and spent about a month with him on the island of St. John. Lisa wanted to get married, but I stalled as long as I could. On our last day there, the final on my divorce from my previous wife came through, and I ended up getting married to the crazy redhead sometime in April on St. Thomas.

I worked my way out to the Redneck Riviera in Alabama and performed around there quite a bit. We went to Minnesota in the summer to visit family and friends. I revisited some of my old haunts and did a bunch of shows up that way. I enjoyed doing some hunting and fishing and had some good times when I was back north. Heading down south again wasn't too much fun, as Lisa and I had a big bust-up at Christmas.

One time we were heading to Bradenton near Palmetto, Florida. We were driving along the highway, and all of a sudden, we heard a big "clunk." Marilyn simply stopped running, and I coasted to a stop on the side of the road. I called a tow truck that pulled her into Palmetto. There, we found out that a rod had broken and rammed through the block of the engine. Poor Marylin! Not knowing what to do, I asked the guy if he could rebuild the motor. He said he could, but it would take some time. I told him to go ahead and tear her down to see what he could do. I would keep in contact with him. I told him that I had to get to Key West, so we loaded everything up onto the Greyhound bus, and we rode to the Keys from Central Florida.

We needed a vehicle, so we went to a used car lot once we hit Key West. I told the salesman, "I only have 100 dollars in my pocket. What do you got? I just need something for the winter to get me around the island."

He pulled out his papers and started to flip through them. He kept mumbling to himself, "No, no, nothing," when all of a sudden, he said, "Here's one for 100 dollars. It's a 280SE Mercedes Benz for 100 dollars."

It was from '65 or '66, but I didn't care what year it was. I told him, "I'll take it if it makes it till the end of the test drive." Off we went, and the car worked great. I gave him a hundred bucks, and I had me a Mercedes! It was in perfect condition but had a lot of miles on it and a little bit of rust on the trunk. Other than that, it was fine. We ended up living in that car during that winter in Key West. Rather than hide at the airport, we got a little campsite that year and set up a small tent.

This was the year of Halley's Comet and my brother came to visit. The comet was in the sky all winter long, and it was gorgeous. It was absolutely stunning to gaze upon those clear nights in Key West! Another friend, a guy by the name of Pete Krogseng, also came down from Minnesota that year. We spent some time showing him the sights. He partied for a couple of weeks with us. This was also the year I began having some difficulties in the relationship with Lisa.

I ran that Mercedes all over Key West that season. I drove it back to the Gulf Coast to see my soon to be ex-wife. Lisa had gone back to her parents' home earlier because she had behaved indiscreetly while I was away playing. I think she fooled around. Of course, I wasn't happy about it, so the Mercedes went back and forth across Florida a couple of times. The Mercedes couldn't handle much speed on the highway, so whenever I got it up to about 60 miles an hour, it would started cutting out. I could hear that it was missing one of its six cylinders. I kept driving, and then heard another cylinder missing. I stopped and checked the oil. There was plenty of it, so I fired it up again. As the car got up to speed, it started missing more cylinders. After about 50 miles, the Mercedes completely gave out. I pulled a spark plug and saw that oil coated the thing.

I knew that there was something seriously wrong if oil was getting into the combustion chamber. I pulled all the plugs, and they were all covered. I cleaned them all off and stuck them back into the engine. I got the car rolling, but after another 50 miles, she started to do the same thing again. When it gave out this time, I went through the routine with the spark plugs and ran another 50 miles. That was a hell of a way to do a road trip. The Mercedes finally limped all the way back to Pensacola with us stopping every 50 miles or so to clean the plugs. It was an 800-mile trip, and it took me an entire day to cover it while giving constant first aid to the Mercedes.

I got to Pensacola and, about four in the morning, broke down in the middle of a traffic intersection. A cop stopped and helped me push the Mercedes to the side of the road so it woulldn't block the intersection. I cleaned the spark plugs again and continued toward the Gulf Coast. When I made it to the redhead's family home, my father-in-law said, "Obviously, there's a crack in the block, and oil is getting into the engine area. It's probably too much money to repair an automobile of this age. You're going to have to put a whole new motor in it. Who knows what else will go wrong with it after that. My suggestion is to get rid of it if you can."

My father-in-law made sense so I took all the spark plugs out, cleaned them off, and put them all back. One of the plugs was stripped, so I smeared some JB weld on it and jammed it into the engine. I waited a day for it to harden, fired the car up, and took it to the used car lot in Foley, Alabama. I sold it to the car lot for $500. I had ridden that thing all over the Keys and Florida that season and still made a $400 profit—on a car with a cracked block! It was time to go shopping for another ride.

These stories about my vehicles help me connect with a lot of the events of my touring life. I didn't use any big tour bus, just a bunch of hardy vehicles sometimes held together with spit and duct tape. These vehicles were a very important part of my life on the road.

My life as an itinerate blues musician from the past acquainted me with many great blues people. One I remember hearing about was Robert Johnson, the great blues musician who, at 27, was poisoned and killed in Mississippi. He was playing in a little barrelhouse and singing to the women at the bar. It turned out that the bar owner's girl was one of the women. The bar owner mixed some rat poison into whiskey and put it in Robert's drink. The next thing you know, Robert's dead because he was messing around with the wrong woman in the wrong place at the wrong time.

In a way, the story about Johnson's murder has some similarities to how I hooked up with the crazy redhead who was the boss' girlfriend at the Flora-Bama. But I managed to slide out of there with her and had the good fortune of not ending up dead. He didn't kill me with no rat-poisoned whiskey, but I did get my second ex-wife out of the deal! I'll talk a bit more about Lisa in the later chapter devoted to the women in my life.

I bought a big old Jeep pickup 4x4 that turned out to be a piece of shit. I got back up north somehow that summer and played gigs, fished, and generally had a good time. When I headed south for the winter, with the marriage deader than a fish left on the dock, I decided to settle a little further north in Alabama and further away from my second ex-wife. I started working around central Alabama, finding gigs from Montgomery to Birmingham.

6

My Time with Johnny Shines

So, there I was, single and divorced again, kicking around Alabama playing all over. I still did lots of gigs all up and down the Gulf Coast, but this turned out to be a major moment in my career because I was playing in many different spots and some of the biggest cities in Alabama. As had been my pattern for several years, I headed north in the summer, playing my way back up to Minnesota. By 1988, I was beginning to develop a bit of a reputation for this blues thing. I had mostly played acoustic Delta blues throughout the mid-'80s.

At some point, I found myself looking through some very old Living Blues magazines, published by the University of Mississippi in Oxford. This magazine was, and still is, the premier blues publication. It covered many traditional Black blues artists and contained articles about musicians, record reviews, and such. As I was digging through my old copies, I saw an article about Johnny Shines.

Now Johnny Shines was a blues singer born in Tennessee back in 1915. He made his base in Chicago for many years and was a well-known member of the blues scene there. Johnny was also famous for being the last traveling companion of the legendary Robert Johnson, who was probably the biggest influence on my music, and especially, my playing as a solo artist.

The article said that Johnny was playing at a festival in Alabama in a small town named Eutaw, which is near Selma. It also said he was a resident of Alabama, which made me wonder exactly where he lived. When I was back in Tuscaloosa playing at Egan's Bar, a couple I knew told me that Shines actually lived in Tuscaloosa! Of course, I was ecstatic to hear that because I wanted to find him. Later, I was partying into the night with a good friend of mine, Cal Woodard, and his band. I mentioned to Cal that Johnny Shines lived in Tuscaloosa. He said, "Let's look him up in the phonebook." We did, and there it was, "J Shines."

I called him up and a woman answered the phone. When I asked if Johnny Shines lived there, she said that he did. I asked if it would be okay if I came over and visited with him, and she said that would be fine. I got his address and went to find him. There were some pretty rundown old houses, and I parked in front of a place I thought was Johnny Shines' house. When I knocked on the door, a Black woman in her early 40s—she turned out to be Johnny's wife, Candy—opened the door. She invited me in and Johnny Shines was sitting right there on the sofa.

You can imagine my excitement to find that this treasure of a bluesman, this living legend, was still alive! I went in and sat with Johnny and we talked about the blues. I told him that I'd read that his birthday was April 26.

He said, "No, boy, that's not right."

I said, "Well, when is your birthday?"

Johnny Shines said, "April 25."

Of course, I was now over the moon because my birthday is April 25, too! He was born in '15, and I was born in '51, so the stars were aligning. I told him, "Sam Charters wrote a book called The Country Blues, and he said that your birthday was April 26."

He stopped me and said, "Boy, Sam Charters don't know nothing about the blues. What does he know about the blues? He never rode in a boxcar or saw a man get shot. He never had to steal chickens to feed his family. He don't know nothing about the blues!"

Johnny was pretty riled about this mistake, but I apologized and told him how excited I was that we had the same birthday. I said that maybe I could throw him a little "Wang Dang Doodle" birthday party and he got a kick out of that. When I got out LeadBessie, my old steel guitar, Johnny was excited to see that I had a National steel guitar. He banged away a little bit on it, and I could see he was struggling because she's not the easiest gal to get along with.

He asked, "You got another one, boy? I've been looking."

I answered, "No, but I'll keep my eyes open for you. If I find one, I'll let you know." After that, we talked some about the old blues musicians and his days with Robert Johnson. Before I left, I asked Johnny, "Would you be interested in doing some shows with me?"

He said, "Yeah, but I can't play like I used to."

I said, "Well, nobody expects you to play like you used to, Johnny. You're 73 years old!"

He said, "Boy, you don't understand. I had a stroke. I can't play my guitar like I used to. I can't hold the strings down properly. It's kind of embarrassing for me."

"Johnny," I said, "you know what I'll do. I'll set you up onstage, get your guitar and all the equipment that you need." I told him that I'd rehearse and practice all the background stuff and would fill the room with sound rhythm and bass sounds—all he'd have to do was sit up there and use his slide. "Slide up and down and sing a few songs. I don't make much money, but whatever you want, you can have. I can get some t-shirts printed up for you and get the recordings from the albums where the record guys ripped you off. We can sell those at the shows, and you can have all the money from that. I've got lots of shows around, including here in your hometown. What do you think?"

He thought a minute and said, "Well, boy, that sounds good, but you've just got me really suspicious. I'm wondering what this white boy wants?"

"Johnny, I wanna hear the stories of the old days. What it was like with you and Robert Johnson, Elmore James, and Muddy Waters and all the other cats who ran the roads down in Mississippi during the early blues days. That's what I want to hear about, and I'll treat you right. I'll feed you and pick you up whatever you want to drink. You do a few songs, tell a few stories, take the money, and off we go. On top of that, I'll take you fishing every day."

"Fishing? Every day?" Johnny asked.

"Yeah, I love to fish, and I got lots of cool spots I'd love to take you to."

With that, we were off and running. I didn't know it at the time, but this would be the beginning of the richest musical relationship of my life and a three-year journey that'd take me all across North America. Johnny and I started doing shows and I took him to some of the most pristine fishing spots around. Eventually, word got out that Johnny Shines was back on the scene and promoters started flying us all over the country to the biggest blues festivals. It was absolute magic! We fished, hunted, rambled, and times were good.

I also secured a several-thousand-dollar grant for Johnny from the Alabama Council of the Arts so that I could study under him. I kept a little bit of it and gave the rest to Johnny. This was extra money for him in addition to everything we pulled in from concerts and selling merchandise. As we went from gig to gig and to festivals, I did what I said I would do. I got some recordings of him, made Johnny some t-shirts, and made a little money as we traveled around. It was great when others realized that Johnny Shines was back doing music because he was well connected with everyone.

Johnny was very proud of his music and played it with joy each night at our shows. He also did a lot of Robert Johnson's songs since that was his old buddy and his big connection with the blues. People would come to him and ask him to play some BB King, Freddy King or Howlin' Wolf. Johnny used to say, "When BB King plays Johnny Shines, Johnny Shines will play BB King."

One night when we were traveling to Auburn from Tuscaloosa to perform, I played a Howlin' Wolf cassette tape. As often happened when I put a blues player in the tape deck, Johnny would start reminiscing about that particular artist. I think we were playing at a place called the Supper Club in Auburn, and when we got to the gig, Johnny sang one of those Howlin' Wolf songs. He only ever did that the one time, but it was impressive. He could imitate Wolf quite well and topped the song off with a beautiful howl.

There was another night I opened for Johnny and played Come into My Kitchen, which is a Robert Johnson song. It's a mellow, "sitting on top of the world" style of a song that Robert wrote and that night, I played it a little slower than normal. When I got off the stage, Johnny said, "Kent, you played that pretty slow tonight."

I said, "Johnny, that's just the way I was feeling it."

He responded, "You know when you played that, I started thinking back about Robert when I first heard that song in St. Louis back in the '30s."

Johnny saying that made me feel like I could inspire him to connect with the music that I loved. It was great to bring Robert Johnson's music back to an audience and to bring Johnny Shines and his music to them, too. I learned all about Robert Johnson from Johnny. He told me how much he admired Johnson and how, when he was in his late teens or early 20s, he wanted to figure out how to play like Johnson. Stories like that reminded me that I was in a very prestigious position.

From time to time, Johnny used to doze off when we were performing. It never bothered me. I figured the man was in his 70s and had had a long day. I mentioned it to him one night. "Johnny, I noticed you dozed off." He said, "Yeah, that music really relaxes me. Don't take offense to it. If you can put me to sleep playing that blues, you're doing your job." That was another nice compliment from old Johnny.

Over time, Johnny got stronger and stronger from all the playing. His profile had risen immensely, and he was getting lots of offers. He had a pocketful of cash and a freezer full of fish. You never saw a happier old bluesman!

During many of our early gigs, I didn't make much money, if any. I always put merchandise out for sale. I had cassettes and t-shirts at the time, so I wasn't too worried about money. For me, it was just an honor to be able to share the stage with Johnny and I'd told him that he could keep most of what we made from the get-go. I printed up Johnny Shines t-shirts, made cassette recordings of his early albums, and produced a few cassettes of Johnny and me playing live in different clubs around the area. We split the money from that and I had plenty of other gigs that I couldn't get Johnny booked on, so I was doing all right.

One evening towards the end of that first year, I was over at Johnny's house just to hang out and talk. He and his wife were sitting at the table playing cards when I came in. Johnny looked up at me and said, "Kent, we gotta talk."

I wondered what was up. I thought maybe he wanted to get rid of me and start doing things on his own or with others. Instead, he said, "I've been talking with my wife here, and we think that God sent you to us. You're a gift from God."

I said, "What's up with that, Johnny? That's pretty heavy."

He said, "Before you came along, I was sitting here with no money. I'd had a stroke, couldn't play my guitar, and things were looking pretty bad. We didn't have much food in the fridge and no cash coming in. You came along, and I'm getting stronger from all this playing. I got a pocketful of money now and my freezer's full of fish. I've got lots of gigs coming in and things are looking great. I feel that God took away my talents by causing the stroke because without the business, I couldn't make a decent living. Then you came along and all of a sudden, I'm renewed. We think you're a gift from God."

I said, "Praise the Lord! Hallelujah!"

He continued. "From now on, we're gonna start splitting the money 50-50." Well, I really whooped it up at that, and that's exactly what we did from then on. Just goes to show you what an honest, fair, and kind old bluesman Johnny Shines was.

Our travels continued and around 1990 we had the opportunity to go to Texas and record an album with harmonica player Snooky Pryor. Snooky was old friends with Johnny from the Chicago days and the sweetest guy you'd want to meet. John Nicholas was producing and playing on the recording. I don't know if John felt a little threatened by me being there, but a couple of other producers for the Blind Pig Record Label went to Johnny and said, "We don't want Kent playing on the recording."

Johnny said, "Well, if I want Kent to play on the recording, Kent plays on the recording."

They answered with, "Well, we'll give him two or three songs to play then."

There was a bit of conflict there, and later that evening, we were in the studio. One of the producers came up and told Johnny that they didn't want him playing guitar on the recording because his stroke subdued his playing. He hadn't quite gotten back to his potential after having the stroke. His playing still had a certain quality to it that was beautiful, but they didn't seem to appreciate that. Johnny looked at me and said, "Kent, I'm just about ready to pull out of here!" We did hang in there to do the recording, and it was a great success. I had a wonderful time hanging out with old Snooky Pryor and listening to his profoundly beautiful harmonica playing. He'd spent a lot of time with Johnny in the early '40s and was one of the founding fathers of that old Chicago blues style; I loved the guy.

It was during that trip to Texas that Johnny wanted us to stop and get some alligator! We were running through Cajun country outside of New Orleans and spotted a Cajun place, so we pulled in. Sure enough, they had alligator on the menu—also rattlesnake, lizard, and other kinds of exotic, weird stuff. Johnny ordered a big sampler plate that featured alligator, snake, lizard, turtle, and other Cajun delicacies. Unfortunately, this meal stopped him up pretty bad. I mean, he couldn't make things happen in the toilet for three or four days. When he was singing one of his songs on the recording, he made a reference to having the "Brownsville Blues." Brownsville is right there on the border of Texas and Louisiana, where we had stopped for his constipating meal.

In our travels, Chicago became an unofficial boundary to our eastern swings, but we had some great times there, playing at Rosa's and at the Chicago Blues Fest. I got to hang out and perform with Sunnyland Slim, who was an old friend of Johnny's. I also performed with Louis and David Myers, the two Myers boys who played with Little Walter and the Aces. Louis played guitar and was fabulous, but David had

had a stroke and couldn't play his bass anymore. We even went over to Pinetop Perkins' house for dinner one night. Johnny just had this deep connection with all the old blues cats, especially the ones from Chicago.

One of the great joys from my years with Johnny was our annual "Wang Dang Doodle Birthday Bash." Since we had the same birthday, each year we'd put together a huge celebration and invite whoever was around to participate. It was always one hell of a fun gig to do together. I'd print up new t-shirts each year and we threw this party three years in a row!

In '91, Johnny and I played the Memphis in May International Music Festival; we were on the bill with Champion Jack Dupree, a great blues player, and Junior Wells. The headliners were BB King and Jeff Healy. We hung out some with Lafayette Leake, who was quite the character and a fabulous blues piano player. He used to sit at the piano and say, "One song, one drink!" He'd have the glasses lined up on top of his piano, waiting for him to drink them down. Lafayette had a Swedish guy playing guitar as his backup. One time after Johnny and I had finished our set, Lafayette asked me to come up and join him. I politely declined, and Johnny got upset about it.

I asked, "What's up, John?"

Johnny said, "You're my boy, and I want you to do me proud. You shoulda gone up there and played."

I felt very bad about this because I thought I'd be disrespecting Johnny by going up and playing with some other blues musician. I thought I was doing Johnny proud by hanging back. Lesson learned. It would have made Johnny look good if his boy got up there and played with Lafayette. I would love to have done it, too, and later apologized to the great pianist.

Later that night, we went backstage to hang out with the legendary BB King. After the show, Johnny and I rode golf carts with BB down Beale Street to the grand opening of his new blues club, which is still in business today. I actually had a chance to jam with BB King that night, but since I didn't have my guitar with me, I had to decline that offer, too. I'm not sure if that upset Johnny or not, but it was another missed opportunity for me.

One of the mysteries of traveling with Johnny was that he was always very nervous whenever we were in Memphis and couldn't wait to get the hell out of there. I don't know if he had somebody gunning for him or if he had some outstanding warrants from the past. He always breathed a sigh of relief when we left that city, though. I never managed to get the full story on that situation.

The summer of '91, we did a prestigious Smithsonian Festival in Washington, D.C. that marked the 25th anniversary of the festival. It was mostly Indonesian art, but the theme for the portion that we were in was "The Roots of Rhythm and Blues: The Robert Johnson Era." We were invited to perform for ten days on the Mall in Washington. A couple of folklore experts connected with the Smithsonian gathered up all these old blues cats from Mississippi and Alabama and took us to the festival. They also invited people from up north connected with Robert Johnson to come and perform.

It was fabulous! All these old blues cats were contemporaries of Robert Johnson. Johnny Shines was the name connection, so I felt like a little "Prince of the Blues" amongst all these guys. Robert Lockwood, whom Robert Johnson taught to play guitar, was there. So was Henry Townsend, a great St. Louis piano player who knew Johnson. We also had Honeyboy Edwards, a cool, old cat from Chicago that was with Johnson the night he was poisoned.

Every day when the festival was getting ready to close, minor players like me played. Every evening or late afternoon, I would get to play a few songs. About the fourth or fifth afternoon, one of the folklorists, Worth Long, came and asked if I'd play my voodoo song for the crowd. You see, I'd written a song about voodoo searching for love. I'd written it on the full moon lunar eclipse on the anniversary of Robert Johnson's death a few years earlier. It went over very well; the crowd loved it.

I found out the next day that the festival's head folklorist went to Johnny and told him that the music I was playing wasn't blues. He wanted to restrict me from performing solo from then on. Though I said, "Okay," it was upsetting because the other folklorists thought the connection was there. Unfortunately, though, the head guy didn't like it so I was out. That was a disappointment.

Later during the festival, one of the other folklorists came to me and said, "Kent, we need your help. The recording with Robert Lockwood, Johnny Shines, Henry Townsend, and Lonnie Pitchford is a little weak, and we want you to dub in some guitar playing." I said I would and did a little rearranging of the music score. I felt pretty good about going over the music and writing notes so Henry Townsend could come in and play some piano lead. It was a little retribution for me that they thought I was worthy of helping to fix up this recording. I got to go inside the Smithsonian recording studio, which was pretty cool, to do this overdub. The end result was a Grammy-nominated record that came out of the Smithsonian Folklife Festival. It was really an honor to be a part of that festival and have some of my music played and stored in the Smithsonian Institute.

The three years I spent with Johnny Shines were the best in my musical life. Over that period, Johnny and I wound up playing over 200 shows together all over the U.S. He passed away in Tuscaloosa, Alabama, on April 21, 1992, at the age of 76. On that day I lost a fellow bluesman, a fishing buddy, a collaborator, a mentor, and most of all, a friend. I'll always be grateful for the many lessons about music and life that Johnny taught me.

Shortly after he passed away, Johnny Shines was inducted into the Blues Hall of Fame. He also won a W.C. Handy Award (now called the Blues Music Awards) from the Blues Foundation for his work on the album with Snooky Pryor that we'd recorded in Texas a couple of years before. These, and other posthumous accolades, were great honors. I only wish Johnny had been around to witness them himself, as I know he'd have gotten a kick out of the recognition.

7

Life on the Lake and Overseas

When Johnny and I played the Smithsonian Festival in Washington, D.C., in the summer of 1991, I wound up meeting the woman who'd become my third wife, Sheri Baker. I invited her out to Minnesota after the festival to enjoy some Northwoods action. She did come out and we partied for three or four weeks up in my old stomping grounds. When she went back south to the D.C. area, I offered to stop by when heading down that way again.

She eventually went to Texas, where she was attending one of the universities there. She invited me to come down, and we hooked up. Before I knew it, she was on the road with me heading back to Alabama, and we ended up living together.

When Johnny Shines died in 1992, it felt like I fell off a cliff. We had been scheduled to play in Lugano, Switzerland, for a big festival called the Blues to Bop Festival. After the funeral, I contacted the promoter and told him that Johnny was gone. I told him we couldn't do the show, but I'd be happy to come and play if he wanted me to. He said, "Yes, come on over," and that is how I made my first trip to Europe.

It was summer in late August, and my soon-to-be wife Sheri and I traveled to Switzerland. We rented a car and proceeded to drive for 10,000 miles through all the countries in western and southern Europe. We even drove to Africa!

The show itself was great! I certainly had an incredible time and met a cool dude named Robert Tilling. He was the Master of Ceremonies at the festival, and he introduced me to the festival's promoter, Norman Hewitt. Norm took me to Italy and introduced me to Gian Carlo Trenti, who was a blues lover from northern Italy. He had a festival he was promoting as well as a company he started called Slang Music. He wanted to push the blues and started bringing blues musicians over to Italy.

He booked me, and I found myself back in Italy in April 1993 to play several shows. I also connected with two British blues festivals, and told the promoters for each that I'd come and play for free if they would let me sell my CDs. If they liked my music, then they could hire me the following year for a full fee. Both of them agreed to the deal.

Sheri and I drove to Italy and then to Britain to play the two festivals. Those events opened the doors to Great Britain for me. The Brits loved the old-style blues connection I had with Johnny Shines. While there, I met a guy who had a music agency in the Dusseldorf area of Germany. Looking back, it seems that I found out about that agency from a man named Rock Bottom. He was a very special guy and one of the most generous musicians I'd ever met. He would pass along information about where to play, who to contact, and, basically, who was who in the music scene across all of Europe. He had an enormous number of contacts from his years in the business and was the reason I met Wolfgang Pieker, who had me performing throughout Germany.

After that, I moved on to a couple of festivals in Scandinavia. One was a well-known one called the Notodden Blues Festival, and it continues to this day. Sheri and I went from Germany to Norway. Unfortunately, we arrived several hours later than scheduled, so the festival canceled my performance. My promoter told me to talk to a guy in Lillehammer who ran a smaller blues festival. I met him and he booked me for the Lillehammer Festival. That opened the door for me in Norway and the rest of Scandinavia.

In 1994, I played the Lillehammer Festival. The blues was just starting to spread around Norway, and the Norwegians were beginning to think about organizing blues clubs in some of the bigger towns. I met a guy who started a music agency called Hell Booking. Hell was the name of the city where he lived, outside of Stjørdal. It's a tiny little place that has a railroad station. From there we started busting through Norway, playing gigs all over.

Norway became a real foothold for me in Scandinavia. Hell Booking arranged many gigs, and over time, I've probably done a decade's worth of tours throughout the country; I had at least one or two big tours every year there. The gigs were mostly during the summertime when the skies were lit from dawn to dawn. Like Alaska, it was the land of the midnight sun. On the other hand, there were a few times I toured there in the dead of winter when there was hardly any sun ever. With so many shows, I developed a wonderful relationship with the Norwegian blues audiences. I had memorable experiences in Norway and still love going back there.

Back in the United States, I married Sheri Baker, wife number three. We bought a big 28-foot travel-trailer and used our new ride to travel to Alaska and back down through British Columbia. It was a fabulous, brand-new truck with no breakdowns and lots of power. I had always wanted to go to British Columbia because of the fishing. Old Outdoor Life magazines featured stories about a place called Kispiox whose streams had giant steelhead trout.

Visiting that area had always been one of my fishing fantasies, and while I was in Norway, I got a notice from my wife that someplace called the Kispiox River Lodge had contacted us about the Kispiox Music Festival; they wanted me to headline. This would have been a dream come true. Unfortunately, the festival was in June or early July.

I contacted them and said, "Look, I'd love to come and play your festival, but it's over 3,000 miles from Alabama." I told them I would work my way up to Montana and do some shows there. Then I'd come to Kispiox and play my show for free if they'd cover my expenses. The other condition I added was that I could come back in September, and guides from the river would show me the ropes for fishing the steelhead. They went for the deal, and it was fabulous. I caught lots of big steelheads and had a great time spending more than a month up and down the river system. The people there were wonderful. I fell in love with the area and wanted to buy land and move up there. I thought about having a blues shack down by the river so that I could come back to the incredible wilderness around the town. However, I had a wife who didn't relish the idea of living in the Canadian wilderness. In fact, she wanted a house in Alabama, so we began looking for property. I thought I had enough money to invest in a home.

We searched all over Alabama for a lake home. Nothing we found was suitable and prices were too high. We decided to move to Georgia where the prices were a bit lower. We ended up on Lake Eufaula, which borders Georgia and Alabama. Here, there were plenty of places that looked pretty cool that might be in our price range. We shopped around and found a place on the Georgia side of the lake. We worked a deal with the owners; we would purchase the property and pay for it with three payments over the span of a year. Finally, we would own a home.

I had planned a tour of New Zealand, then Australia to open doors there. Instead, I ended up booking a colossal nine-week tour in Norway. The cash from that tour was enough to make the first house payment and we were able to move in. I had two more payments to make, so I booked more tours overseas. I hit Britain, Norway again, Italy, France, and Germany and worked my tail off. After a year, I'd paid for the house.

It was the mid-'90s and things were going well overseas. I was making some real money, and banking it. As a result, we were living in a wonderful home on a beautiful blue lake. Life was good. I even stopped doing my autumn fishing up in British Columbia because it was so beautiful on Lake Eufaula at that time of the year. I wanted to stay at home and enjoy it.

I was doing all kinds of touring in the late 1990s when, suddenly, European money started to drop in value. All over the continent, European currencies fell by half against the dollar. When it hit rock bottom, I was making about half of what I used to in US dollars. Of course, they weren't going to pay me more because they weren't using dollars. Therefore, I kind of had to switch up a little bit and didn't work in Europe for a while. Later, as their economy improved, I started doing some gigs again in Britain and Scandinavia. When you make music for a living, you don't think much about international economics, but it sure can affect you significantly if you work abroad. It was a crash course for me in currency exchange rates and figuring out how much money I would actually make when I came home after playing a club in Rome.

Overall, the late '90s were a good time; things were flowing. I worked hard, made good money, had the house paid off, and I was earning enough to pay the bills. I was touring overseas, working around the South and also making yearly trips to Minnesota to visit my parents who were getting older.

As we slid into a new century, I was still living in that little spot on Lake Eufaula. I guess things were going well, as I was still married to wife number three. Unfortunately, Sheri wasn't getting along well with our neighbors, so she decided that we needed to look for another place to live. I wasn't very happy about it because I was satisfied with where we were. However, I tried to be fair to her, and we started looking to relocate. Soon, we found some land on the lake further down from where we were living and decided to buy a couple of one-acre lots.

We were going to build a house on this double lot in the woods on a hill with about 300 feet of lakeshore. It wasn't my first choice of what to do with my time, but I agreed. We started clearing the land, and I researched how to build a house. I'd never built anything in my life that wasn't a disaster, but I began studying building techniques and came up with a design. Planning to build the house on this hill we now owned, I had a geologist come out and examine the site to ensure that we could build there. I didn't want to construct the thing and have it wash down the hill during the first big rainstorm, as the area is known for "providence sand," which is sand that will shift with water erosion.

I got the okay to build and continued clearing the land myself. Next, I started building a foundation, and that went nicely. I began looking for wood to construct the house with, but a lot of my money was tied up in buying the lots over five years. The purchase was a good deal at the time, but it certainly squeezed the budget. I started going overseas to do shows in order to save up for building supplies.

Back in the States, while scouting for supplies, I found an old house in a scrap yard recycler in Columbus, Georgia. It had Douglas fir timbers and, according to some of the stamps still on the timber, the wood was from virgin timber shipped down from Canada. I bought that house and used most of the wood from it. Dump trucks came out 70 miles to my building site and dumped all this used wood in my yard. I had three huge piles of timbers. There were some big pieces that were 30, 20, and 15 feet long. I also literally had hundred or more pieces that were 3"x 9" and ran 8 to 32 feet long. I even had about five miles of Douglas fir tongue-and-groove flooring. Sheri and I spent close to six months pulling out nails and sanding wood. We stripped any lumber that was painted and planed it smooth. We refinished it with turpentine and linseed oil.

It was absolutely gorgeous wood, and I started building, studying construction and learning about construction slenderness ratios. The plan was to build in the style of old American barns by using pegs and different joints for putting the building together. I studied all the joints and notching techniques and decided that it was too much for me. It would have taken years to learn that notching style properly.

I didn't have the manpower to lift an entirely constructed wall at one time, so I decided to go with a post and beam style with principled rafters, steel plates, and bolts. I designed it that way so that I could build it myself. The house ended up close to 3,000 square feet with three floors, counting the loft. It was an open floor plan with a cathedral ceiling, and I thought it turned out fabulously.

Even now, when I'm in Great Britain, I joke with my audiences that I call my home the "House the Brits Built" because my gigs there did a lot of the financing. They all get a big kick out of that. I always invite them all to come over for a visit. It still needs finishing, but I built it pretty much all by myself. Sheri helped with some of the work and so did my eventual fourth wife, Sarah, but I did most of it. I found ways to move massive beams myself and it took a lot of effort. It was all worth it, though, as I still have a beautiful house on Lake Eufaula.

Left: Famous Piedmont blues player John Jackson in 1970.

Below: Willie Dixon at the Caboose in the early '70s.

Above: Photo I took of Muddy Waters in 1972.

Right: Kim Wilson and I onstage in Minnesota in the early '70s.

Below: Johnny Shines and I at the Alabama Music Hall of Fame grand opening ceremony, 1990.

Johnny and I playing WC Handy's porch in Florence, Alabama.

Above: A special moment with two steel guitars at Egans in Tuscaloosa, 1989.

Below: Fishin' buddies after a successful day in Minnesota.

Above: Jammin' with Tommy Burns at Egans.

Below: Johnny and I with Snooky Pryor.

Above: With John Hammond Jr. (center) at the Edmonton Folk Fest in 1991.

Below: Sunnyland Slim, Johnny Shines, and Chicago Bob Nelson.

Above: Johnny and Pinetop Perkins in Chicago, 1991.

Below: Johnny between Lewis and David Myers from The Aces.

Above: Johnny and I with Fingers Taylor.

Below: With Mama Rosa at her popular Chicago blues lounge.

Above: With Mama Rosa's son, Tony M.

Below: With Kim Wilson in 1991.

Above: The fishin' musicians outside of Auburn, AL.

Above: With Robert Jr. Lockwood at the 1991 Smithsonian Festival of American Folklife honoring The Robert Johnson Era.

Below Left: Me with Jessie May Hemphill.

Below Right: With Ruth Brown.

Above: My family hanging out with Johnny in Minnesota.

Below Left: Robert Johnson Festival flyer commemorating Johnny Shines.

At the Gloucester Blues Festival in the UK, 1993. (Courtesy Tim Spencer)

Frank Ross with Leadbessie at the Chicago Blues Festival.

Right: Posing with Leadbessie at The Pit Music Venue in the UK, 1993. (Courtesy Tim Spencer)

Below: Back again playing the Gloucester Blues Festival, 1994. (Courtesy Tim Spencer)

Above: Legendary blues pianist, Pinetop Perkins, on my guitar

Below: Kim Wilson and I in the mid-'90s.

Above: Me and my French connection at Les Lou in the mid-'90s.

Right: With John Mooney in San Francisco.

Above: Stolen Blues Old Stand sign given to me by the band of same name.

Below: Rare moment with an L5.

Jamming at the Wrotham Arms Public House in the UK, 2019. (Courtesy Tim Spencer)

8

University of Minnesota Blues and Leadbessie

A long list of incredible blues cats came through to play the University of Minnesota back in the late '60s and early '70s. I got to see Mance Lipscomb, Sleepy John Estes with Hammie Nixon, Johnny Shines, Mississippi Fred McDowell, Big Joe Williams, and Bukka White—to name just a few. The school had put together a blues series that brought in many blues players mainly from the South, but there were some from other parts of the country, too.

Mississippi Fred McDowell, a famous slide guitar player, gave a seminar that I went to. I sat right next to him as he was talking about his music. It was exciting, but there were only a handful of people there, which surprised me. I was fascinated with his playing because he kept his thumb moving all the time, chunking away at the bass line. It was a pattern that I was struggling with and couldn't figure out. Finally, I asked him, "Hey, could you tell us a little bit about your thumb and the way you work it?"

He looked at me and said, "Sure, boy," and went into an explanation. I couldn't understand a word he was saying!

I felt embarrassed, but said, "Oh, that was great. Thanks." I told myself then and there that this blues thing was probably gonna take some time. Like most any skill worth having, it's most likely going to take you at least ten years to become capable. I reminded myself to be patient because I loved the music and knew that if I kept at it long enough, it might eventually come to me. I never did learn Fred's style, but I loved it. It was such an unusual technique the way he played that slide while keeping his thumb moving all the time.

Fred played beautiful music for the students out in the courtyard later that evening. I was there watching him and realized that playing the blues was what I wanted to do with my life. I spoke about this before, but it really made an impression—he was sitting down and had drinks that fans had bought him lined up all the way across the stage. There was a whole row of beautiful, young girls in the front while he was playing and I told myself that this was the life for me. This is the job I want!

Another guy who had an impact on me was Big Joe Williams. He was something else with his 9-string guitar, which he had made by adding three tuners to the headstock of a regular 6-string. To see and hear him play was an experience any blues lover would cherish.

There was also something that came to town called the Memphis Blues Caravan. It was a group of guys from Memphis who were booked to play in Minnesota at a few different places. I went to a couple of shows and went out with some of the boys like Sleepy John Estes and Hammie Nixon. There was also an old cat named Furry Lewis, who was one of the cool old slide guitar blues cats. I remember Piano Red, an albino Black guy, who played real cool piano.

Houston Stackhouse and the King Biscuit Boys were also part of the Caravan. They had this white guy named Harmonica Frank Floyd, and he played a bluesy country kind of thing on the harp. He was just incredible! It was the first time I ever saw anyone playing harmonica by sticking it all the way inside his mouth and playing it without having to hold the harmonica with his hands.

I also got to see John Jackson and Hound Dog Taylor, who came and played university-sponsored shows. Hound Dog was so good; he was really renowned for his slide playing on electric guitar. Then one night between sets, this young red-headed girl got up and started playing a National steel guitar. She tore it up and I was blown away! Come to find out her name was Bonnie Raitt. This was the early '70s, so she was probably in her early 20s and wasn't yet the world famous musician we know today. But she was really something, even back then.

Big Mama Thornton was another gal who played the blues and came through there. I saw her play in the park at the university. It was also around this time that I got to play with the great harmonica player, Big Walter Horton.

We also had Booker T. Washington "Bukka" White come to town to play at the university. Wayne White and I begged the promoter to give us the opening act, and it worked, so we got to open for Bukka White for both shows he played. This got me backstage with old Bukka and we watched as he sat in the corner just being quiet. A woman from the university was supposed to give him a bottle of whiskey or brandy before each show, and she delivered. He drank the first one down and played a great show. Then she brought another bottle before his second show, and he went to work downing that one.

Bukka was the main guy who inspired me to pursue the steel guitar. He had a National steel guitar from the 1930s and he played bottleneck slide Mississippi Delta blues. He was really a master, and I remember asking if I could play him a little instrumental I'd been working on. It was a bunch of licks that he was known for that I'd picked up off his recordings. He said, "Sure, boy, go ahead and give it a go."

I asked, "Well, do you think it'd be all right if I used your guitar?" He had his National right there and I was dying to get my hands on one to see what they were like to play. I wanted one so bad!

Bukka gave me the OK, and I got to play his National steel guitar backstage at the old coffee house at Coffman Union, University of Minnesota. Since probably about 1967, I'd already been keeping my eye out for one, but the search for a National steel guitar really began in earnest after opening those two shows for Bukka.

The National String Instrument Corporation was formed in 1927 to produce resonator guitars, mandolins and ukuleles. A resonator is an aluminum cone embedded into the face of a guitar that really projects the string vibration and sound beyond what a normal acoustic guitar can deliver. Back then—before the electric guitar had been invented—there was a need for a guitar that wouldn't be drowned out by horns and other instruments when playing in groups, combos and orchestras. National built them to be loud and they became very popular.

There is quite a history of players of differing styles of music playing National steel guitars. They were the choice for so many blues greats like Sister Rosetta Tharpe, Tampa Red, Taj Mahal, John Hammond, and Son House (who was another huge inspiration for me wanting one). But you could also find country, jazz and even Hawaiian-music players using them back in the '20s and '30s when they were being manufactured.

I started looking in all the newspapers wherever I traveled, like the "Want Ads" for used musical instruments. I'd go in all the music stores in whatever town I'd happen to be in while I was traveling around playing music. Over the ten years that I looked for one, never once did I find a National steel guitar just hanging in a music shop to be sold. These things were so hard to find back then. When Bukka White died in early 1977, I was hoping there might be some way I could track down his guitar and get my hands on it, but that wasn't to happen. As a side note, in 2019, Bukka's 1933 National steel guitar sold at auction in Great Britain for $130,000!

Later in 1977, while I was working for my brother up at his resort, I had this friend from Duluth, Minnesota, who was a guitar builder. This guy's name was Greg Nelson and he was an old musician acquaintance of mine and quite a good guitar player. He learned how to build guitars in Minneapolis and then moved up to Duluth to open his own shop, called Nelson Guitars I believe.

Another guitar-playing buddy of mine, Charlie Bingham, called me up outta the blue one day and said, "Hey, Greg's got a steel guitar he just took in on trade!" Charlie knew how hard I'd been looking; Greg did not.

So with this information, I got a 100 dollar bill and put it in my pocket. Greg was a party boy and used to throw them all days of the week. I went over there on a Sunday night and partied with him, trying to play it cool. I started kind of looking around his house and I found a guitar case sitting in his closet. So I casually said, "Hey, Greg, what's that sitting in your closet there?"

He said, "Oh, you haven't seen my steel guitar?"

So I acted surprised like I didn't know and said, "Oh, you got a steel guitar in?"

He said, "Yeah, man."

So I said, "Well, let me see it."

And he opened up that guitar case and I just fell in love: 14-fret, 1934 National Duolian steel guitar. Perfect. So, I sat and played it all night in his bedroom. After a while, Greg came back in and said, "Hey, Kent, aren't you gonna come and join us?"

By then, all my coolness had worn off. I said, "Man, you got this guitar, this steel guitar just sitting in your closet. Greg, I've been looking for a steel guitar for close to 10 years now and you've got one sitting in your closet." I said, "You've got to sell it to me, you've got to." I said, "I promise, if you sell it to me, I'll play it all over the world. And if you don't sell it to me, Greg, I'm gonna have to move in with ya."

So he laughed and said, "Well, OK, I'll sell it to you."

I asked, "How much do you want?"

And if I remember correctly, Greg said, "$700."

And I said, "OK, well I've got $100 here and I'm gonna give you that, and it'll take me a little while to get you the other $600, but I promise I'll get you the money. It might take me a little while, but here's $100 and I'll come back. Don't sell it to anybody else."

And he said, "OK."

And I was thinking, "Oh my goodness!"

So, I was getting ready to leave and he said, "Well, why don't you just go ahead and take the guitar with you."

So, I took it home that night and it's been heaven ever since. I ended up paying him the $700. I think I was making $52 per week (plus room and board) working for my brother, so it took me quite a while to save up the rest. But I did eventually come up with it all and got it to Greg.

One day I was sitting around with my "Skin and Bones" partner, Tommy Burns, and we were talking about a name for the guitar. He said, "Well, why don't you call her LeadBessie?" 'Cause I'd been thinking, "Leadbelly, Leadbelly, Leadbelly." But LeadBessie, that sounded really good to me. You combine Leadbelly with Bessie Smith, and you get LeadBessie. That was the one!

Since then, LeadBessie and I have done more than 10,000 shows and we've traveled over three-million miles. She's actually quite famous. Four and a half wives have come and gone, but me and LeadBessie have never had an argument. She'll be 86 years old in 2020, but I'm hoping to get a few more miles out of her.

She is pretty beat up and she's got lots of duct tape, but all that just gives her more character. I do all the repairs on her myself. I've redone the frets, I've epoxied the neck, epoxied the body, and I've made a few soldering joints on her here and there. But LeadBessie just keeps kicking and I'm really proud of the things we've accomplished together.

9

Muddy Waters and Stevie Ray Vaughan

I first saw Muddy Waters in 1970 in Detroit at the Chess Mate Coffeehouse, where he was playing late one night. I got there and stayed all night long watching him perform. Muddy was singing and playing his heart out and I loved every moment of it! I think he was still recovering from a car wreck that killed his driver. He was all patched up and in some sort of body cast. Muddy was taking a break just as I arrived. I saw where he went, headed that way, and I looked through some swinging doors leading into the kitchen area of the coffee house. Old Muddy was back there plugging down some whiskey or some brandy before he came out to play again.

Not long after that, I saw him again at the Ann Arbor Blues Fest, where he played a fabulous afternoon set. Around that time we'd started having quite a blues happening in the Minneapolis and St. Paul area, so Muddy came to town and played quite a few times. I remember hanging with him backstage one of those occasions when he was playing down in the cellar of a little beer joint called The Silver Dollar Saloon. I remember cozying up to him and trying to get a little bit of his mojo to rub off on this white boy. I finally asked him to give me some tips or a secret about this blues stuff. I was starting to play it and wanted to learn as much as I could from all the longtime blues musicians I met. When I asked the question, Muddy looked at me and said, "Boy, reefer and champagne!" Oh, we partied hardy with old Muddy Waters.

One time a friend of mine was bringing some blues cats, including Muddy, to a club just outside of Minneapolis. I had a photo with me of Muddy from backstage at one of his earlier shows. Another friend had used my camera to get the shot of Muddy's face while he was kind of smirking, and I'd had it blown up to 12 inches by 12 inches. I took it backstage to Muddy and asked if I could have an autograph. He said, "Sure, boy." I laid that big photo down and he looked at it and cracked a huge smile. He said, "Boy, that's me! That's Muddy Waters!" He sounded liked he was sort of surprised and amused by the photo. Maybe he was used to seeing photos of himself up on stage, but not too many that were up close and personal like this one was. He signed it, "To Kent, from Muddy." It hangs in my studio to this day in a position of prestige.

In 1983, Muddy passed away, and I went to his funeral service in Chicago with Ted Wilebski from Wilebski's Blues Saloon. Ted flew us down there to attend the proceedings and to celebrate Muddy's life. When we went to the wake, we stood in line to view Muddy in his coffin; he didn't look so good. He wore the same old suit jacket he'd always worn when performing.

While there, we jammed all around Chicago with some of the cool blues cats of the day. We jammed and partied with

Junior Wells, Lefty Dizz, and Buddy Guy at his club called the Checkerboard, where Muddy had been playing the previous year. There's a video out there with Muddy being joined by the Rolling Stones at the Checkerboard. Late one night, we went to a place called the Kingston Mines and Stevie Ray Vaughan showed up. Stevie was an old acquaintance of mine from the mid-'70s.

Back when I played with Kim Wilson in Aces, Straights, and Shuffles, a friend of his from Texas, Jimmie Vaughan, came up and played guitar with us on a few occasions. Jimmie had a real cool style that was much different than the Chicago style we were playing. He had more of a Texas or Southern shuffle style. When Aces, Straights, and Shuffles broke up, Kim split down to Texas and started The Fabulous Thunderbirds with Jimmie. Later on, whenever I'd find myself in Austin with other bands, we'd always hook up with Kim and Jimmie.

One time they told us about a real happening spot there in Austin called Antone's Blues Club. We checked it out and I remember the first time walking in and seeing Stevie Ray Vaughan playing with Eddie Taylor, who was another great guitarist who'd played a lot of the licks on Jimmy Reed albums. Stevie was this skinny kid standing up there and playing Texas- blues with some fire. You could also really hear the Albert King influence in his playing. I found out later he was a sideman playing in a band called Paul Ray and the Cobras.

I think Jimmie Vaughan was close to my age and Stevie was a few years younger. Stevie could really deliver onstage, but he always seemed fairly shy to me off it, at least back then. Later, after I'd left and come back north, I found out Stevie had started his own band and was touring around. Kim and the Thunderbirds would occasionally come through Minneapolis and we'd always head out to see them, and soon enough Stevie started following that same trail. Whatever gigs The Fabulous Thunderbirds were doing on the road, it seemed like Stevie Ray Vaughan and Double Trouble would be there soon after. So he and I had crossed paths a few times in Minnesota.

Anyway, Stevie showed up that night to the Kingston Mines and it was the first time I'd seen him in a few years. This was 1983 and he was really starting to make some waves in the music business. Just a couple of months after Muddy's funeral, he would release Texas Flood, which would be the album to eventually propel him to household name status. I went over and started talking to Stevie, and soon enough we were all jamming together and taking turns getting up to play a little bit in Muddy's memory. I can't recall what all we played since I was pretty hammered.

Later that night, I remember sitting right next to Buddy Miles, the big drummer who'd played in Jimi Hendrix's Band of Gypsies. I vaguely remember us all leaving with Lefty Dizz, his sister and his girlfriend early in the morning. By then, I didn't know where the hell I was, but I was enjoying the party. Muddy would have been pleased, because he liked to party himself.

Johnny Shines told me that he and Muddy were once standing outside Muddy's apartment in Chicago, and they were both very drunk. Muddy dropped his keys and couldn't even bend over to pick them up without falling, and poor Johnny couldn't help the situation either. He had to call his wife to come out and pick up his keys for him. Like I said, Muddy loved to party!

I play many of Muddy's songs to this day; it's something I've always done and will continue to do. He was the king of Chicago Blues. Actually, Muddy and Howlin' Wolf are probably somewhere duking it out for that title.

Muddy Waters' given name was McKinley Morganfield.

There are quite a few different stories about how old Muddy got his nickname. I originally heard that his grandmother named him that because he was always playing in the muddy water of a creek. He would always come back all dirty and wet, but that might just be a story that went around.

These days, there are two of Muddy's sons playing blues music—Mud Morganfield and Big Bill Morganfield—so it's good that Muddy's legacy lives on in the music world. I'll always appreciate the influence he had on my love for the blues.

10

The Life of "Luxury"

Atraveling musician spends a lot of time in the vehicle it takes to get him from gig to gig. As I look back and try to piece together my crazy life, I'm usually able to figure out the time period that a particular story took place by thinking about what I was driving at the time. The vehicles really help me connect with the events of my life on the road; they become characters in their own right as I'm thinking back.

Since that first '51 Chevy I got at the age of 16, I've owned all manner of cars, trucks, jeeps, and wagons over the years—probably about 25 in all. I've crashed some, others have blown up, some were lemons, and some were excellent. We've already talked about "Marilyn," the Cadillac limo that Tommy Burns and I drove all over the U.S. And I told you about the Mercedes 280SE that I bought for $100, ran into the ground, and sold for $500.

Another vehicle that brings back great memories is

a Dodge Avco motorhome that I bought around 1987 and named "Luxury." I purchased her in Montgomery, Alabama, from some old, retired, service dude. To give you a visual idea of the Avco, it was a Class A motorhome on a chassis supplied by Dodge, and mine was about 30 feet long. The Avco motorhome combined transportation with some of the high-end features of the time, such as a microwave oven. It was a stable ride, built with an eye for comfort and safety. I started running Luxury up and down the roads, from Alabama to Minnesota and back down again.

That motorhome had some crazy size tires. They had tubes and liners, and I was always struggling with them. The tires were forever either going flat or becoming worn out. I had a couple of places where I could get replacements, so I carried lots of spare tires, tubes, and liners with me. I got pretty darn good at changing big RV wheels and tires along the road.

Often we parked Luxury in the club parking lot at Norm's in Birmingham, where I used to play a lot back then. Now, Norm's was just the greatest spot. The boss loved me there, paid me well, and let me plug in at the club. He had all the connections I needed, so I could come back and land there after a gig from anywhere in the state. Norm's was always open until late at night, or rather, early in the morning. I could always party my brains out and then crawl out to the motorhome; just like that, I was home.

I imagine the main reason I still hold such an affinity for Luxury is that it's the vehicle I had while Johnny Shines and I were playing together. Johnny would always ride along in the captain's seat and boy, did we have some times together. We'd do a gig in one part of the state and then drive through the night to the next place. I'd drink a few beers along the way and put some blues music on the stereo. Old Johnny would start reminiscing about Howlin' Wolf, Robert Johnson,

Muddy Waters or John Lee Hooker. Whoever was playing on the stereo brought back memories for Johnny, and he would laugh and tell a funny story. He really liked that motorhome.

Once, Johnny and I had some shows booked up in Minnesota, so we hopped in Luxury and set out. On the way there, Luxury's transmission started acting up. I had a friend in Shannon, Alabama, a mechanic who was working in a transmission shop. After he did some repair work, Johnny and I got back on the road, but we were still 1,200 miles away from Minnesota. We got that thing out of the shop, started driving and managed to get all the way up to north Alabama before we had another problem: Luxury started leaking transmission fluid. It was very stressful to ride down the highway watching transmission fluid oozing out of your motorhome. We limped along for about 100 miles, and that leak kept getting worse and worse. Soon, blue smoke started billowing out the back because the fluid was hitting the exhaust system. Here we were, in a pretty good size vehicle, with this big blue plume of smoke trailing behind us. It was like in the movies when a James Bond-type car lets loose with a smokescreen, but instead of a slick little Aston Martin, it was a damn monstrous motorhome. I'd stop periodically to get more fluid to pour in the engine because we didn't have time to get it repaired and still make it to Minnesota in time for the gigs.

We kept chugging north with our smoke cloud behind us. I remember getting to Chicago on a Sunday morning. The tranny was still smoking like crazy, and I didn't know what to do. I thought maybe we could have somebody take a quick look at it and maybe there might be something they could do to repair it quickly. Well, the only place open on a Sunday morning was a little Sears automotive repair shop. They said that they could look at it later in the day, so I thought, "Okay, we'll park here and wait." I'd been driving all night and had logged in about 18 hours straight. I was tired as hell and told Johnny that I needed to sleep for a couple of hours.

It didn't take long for me to doze off, but Johnny soon woke me up and said, "Kent, we gotta do something. We can't sit here now." I don't know what was going on in Johnny's mind. He must have been nervous about something or another because Johnny was the man! But, whatever he wanted to do was what I was going to do. It didn't matter what else we were dealing with, I went with what Johnny needed.

I got up and we started driving out of Chicago and eventually pulled into a little rest area. I took a couple of chickens out of the refrigerator, lit the stove, stuck the chickens in the oven, and off we went. After about an hour and a half, we could smell that chicken fat sizzling in the pan and it smelled so good. Johnny waited in anticipation. After another thirty minutes, Johnny was licking his lips and darn near drooling from the smell of that chicken. Thirty minutes later, right after we passed Madison, Wisconsin, I pulled off the freeway and asked, "Johnny, you ready to eat?"

He darn near leaped out of his seat and headed for the table. I plopped those two cooked birds down on the table and Johnny and I feasted in Luxury, so to speak. It was a joy watching him eat because he loved his food. He told me later, "Kent, that's the best chicken I've ever eaten in my whole life." Either he was very hungry, or I did a pretty good job with the cooking; having to sit there and smell that wonderful aroma for almost three hours must have driven Johnny crazy. That was a joyful moment in the middle of our smoky ride up to Minnesota. Once we got to my home state, we got the transmission squared away and did a couple of shows. When they were over, we ran up to the Northwoods.

I had a bass boat at the time. It was a Ranger 350V with a 150 horsepower Mercury engine on the back of it. I kept it up in Minnesota and stored it at the house that I owned. Johnny and I zipped in there to pick up the boat. We had some time off, so I took him up to my favorite place in Minnesota, Voyageurs National Park, located on the boundary of Minnesota and Canada. This was the beautiful, wild area where I spent much of my youth with my brothers and father.

Johnny and I stayed in a little resort area that had a campground and I took him out on the water in the bass boat. He got a bit bug-eyed with the speed of the boat and the bounciness of the big waves out there on the lake, but he got through it fine. Johnny was one who never complained much about anything. This trip was a great experience for him; we caught tons of fish, ate well and had a wonderful time.

I remember Johnny and me driving Luxury from Minneapolis up to Big Sandy Lake in the McGregor area, where my parents had a place. It was about a three-hour drive. There's a portion of Tamarack Swamp that goes on for about twenty miles. It's close to Highway 65 where my parents were. We were driving north in the middle of the night. It was beautiful, and I was very excited to get Johnny up there and have him meet my family. Unfortunately, the motorhome blew a front tire. I was going about 65 miles per hour and the vehicle was shaking so bad that I could barely keep hold of the steering wheel. In fact, the vibration made it impossible to see out of the windshield. I looked over at poor Johnny, and his eyes were as big as saucers! I finally got Luxury slowed down, and we pulled over. It was really late, and there was no traffic on the road; I didn't know for sure what we could do about our situation. We were still at least 15 miles from my parents' house, which was too far to walk. I decided to make sure we were off the road and stay put for the night. It was a quiet evening and Johnny decided to go outside and pee. I didn't know if he just wanted some fresh air, but I did say, "You should use the toilet because there are a lot of mosquitoes out there."

Johnny said, "No, I wanna go outside and take a pee."

He went outside, and those mosquitoes were all over him big time! Minnesota is the mosquito capital of the world. I don't care what anyone says, it's the worst, especially in the Tamarack Swamp area. Poor Johnny was trying to pee, and he was swatting and swinging his arms and running. Johnny didn't normally run, but he ran that night back to the motorhome! Poor Johnny came in, and I fogged the place down because I knew that the mosquitoes had followed him in. I looked at him, smiled and said, "Johnny, I told you not to go out there, poor old guy." He was a trooper though.

The next morning I got ready to work on the tire. For some reason, I couldn't get the motorhome jacked up to get the wheel off. We flagged down a trucker who gave us a ride up to where my parents were. I walked in to see them and told them that I broke down along the road. My father took us back to Luxury and helped me get that wheel off. He gave me a special tool that he'd had for years; it was a big wheel lug wrench for truck-style tires. Of course, my dad had this because he had every tool under the sun.

We finally got old Luxury up and running again, and got her to my parents' house. After visiting them, we went up to Big Sandy Lake and did a bunch of fishing. It was a wonderful time. We also went to one of the coolest places ever—the Deer Lake Boogie. The Boogie was a party that friends of mine from radio station KAXE public radio in Grand Rapids, helped promote. The party was held at the Blackmarrs' place on Deer Lake. All these homemade school buses that looked like little cabins on wheels were parked all around. It was a weekend for music lovers and I attended as often as I could during the '80s and '90s. Eventually, I became one of the primary connections for the Boogie.

When I brought Johnny Shines to the Boogie that year, it was the biggest deal on earth for everyone there. He was a legendary bluesman, and the rest of us were just wannabees. All weekend, musicians played different styles of music that were mostly acoustic. To have Johnny Shines on stage was incredible! Johnny loved those people up there. They treated him like gold. It was a totally unpretentious audience made up of cool, hippie kinds of folks who loved live music and the freedom of the Northwoods. Johnny was right there with them!

Old Luxury got us up there, but it wasn't her only trip. Other crazy things happened with that motorhome. I remember her having more transmission trouble. I was back in Alabama with my friend Haz, who worked on a lot of my vehicles over the years. He was an excellent mechanic and a dear friend who decided that the whole transmission needed rebuilding. He and the shop owner, Albert, were willing to let me sit in the parking lot and live in the vehicle while they worked on the tranny. It was going to take some time, and they were going to do it between other projects. They had some big cash customers that they needed to take care of first.

So I could get around while they were repairing the motor home, Haz set me up with a vehicle that I bought for about $500 dollars. It was a beautiful brown Chevy Nova. It had a 350-horsepower motor that one of the crazy rednecks from Shannon, Alabama, owned. I later sold that Nova to Johnny Shines for a little less than I'd paid.

While Luxury was parked at the transmission shop, I remember one incident that made me really mad. There were some old rednecks that had come by and one of them happened to poke his head in my motorhome door. I had a lot of pictures in there, and the first thing he saw was a big picture of Muddy Waters, some photos of Johnny Shines, and some smaller postcard pictures of a bunch of the cool old bluesmen that I had hanging on my wall. "If I'm not mistaken," the redneck said, "this looks like a nigga shack!" I promptly grabbed him and pushed him back toward the door. I held back from smacking him and said, "Get away from my home." He shook his head and walked off. That's the kind of racial bullshit you came across from time to time. You try to be friendly to folks, and they start spewing racist bullshit.

Finally, Haz got old Luxury repaired and running. The motorhome once again became the way to get around and served as a base for gigs and some more exploration of the country.

I remember making runs between Montgomery and Tuscaloosa when we'd be down South. I'd bring Johnny back to Tuscaloosa to his home many times after a late-night show. There was a little barbeque place outside of Tuscaloosa in the countryside called the Twix and Tween. I'm assuming the name had something to do with being in between Tuscaloosa and Centreville. It was right off Highway 82, the "Blues Highway," as we called it. Whenever we traveled that way, Johnny and I had to stop in for several pounds each of smoked pork, Johnny's favorite. By the time we got to Tuscaloosa 20 minutes later, he'd have a pound of it wolfed down and be working on more. He loved that place, and it was always a real pleasurable thing for him to stop late at night and pick up some pulled pork. Good old Johnny!

We took that motorhome out to Mississippi several times. Once, we played a blues show in Jackson, Mississippi, at a place called Hal and Mal's. When we were heading home after that gig, we were nearing Meridian, Mississippi, and I threw my cigarette butt out the window. That was the one and only time I saw Johnny get upset with me. He looked at me and said, "Don't do that. I don't wanna get pulled over by the cops here in Mississippi." I think he was frightened more than he was angry. He was rebuking me for giving the cops any reason to pull us over in that state. The thought made him very nervous and I never threw a cigarette out again.

Maybe a year or two after that incident, the Delta Blues Museum asked us to come and do a fundraiser for them in Jackson, Mississippi. I found out later that they were moving the museum from a library to its own building. We did the fundraiser around 1989 or 1990. Sometime around '91 we went back to Hal and Mal's. I remember the year because my third wife-to-be, Sheri, was with us.

We got to the beautiful Yazoo River Delta area, boogied down the road a ways, and pulled over for the night. I think we were scheduled to play the next day at a festival, and we stopped not far from Greenville. Sheri told me that she couldn't find one of her cats, so I started tearing the place apart looking for it. Her cats were the most important thing on earth. I was about third in line, if that. Johnny wasn't a big fan of cats, but he put up with Sheri's because he was very tolerant.

I couldn't find that cat anywhere despite tearing the place apart. Poor Johnny was trying to sleep and I was crawling around underneath him, digging through everything in the motorhome. When I finally had to tell Sheri that I couldn't find the cat, she said, "Oh, we gotta turn around and go back because she must have jumped out when you guys were out there taking a pee."

I said, "We could turn around and go back, but I don't know exactly where we stopped. There's no guarantee that I can find the place in the middle of the night. Why don't we just run on and tomorrow, we'll get a rental car for you? You can go back and search for her. Johnny and I will play the festival, and then we'll hook up and see if we can find your cat." Oh, man, I tell you that she was not happy about that. We argued some more about it, and I went back to tear through old Luxury again. Thank goodness, I finally found her! She was tucked in behind everything in the cupboard, way back behind the refrigerator jammed into a tiny space. I could see her eyes and nose. I reached in and got the death grip on her and yanked her out. It resolved the situation but, oh, talk about stress and women!

Johnny and I went on to the festival and had a great time. BB King was the headliner, and Albert King was there. Rufus Thomas was the MC. It was a beautiful event, and I got to hang out with Albert King shortly before he passed away. I sat in his truck with him and we talked about life in general and blues and things he liked to do.

Since we had the motorhome, Johnny was nice and comfy when we traveled. We had a generator so that we could run the air conditioner in the hot summer. Johnny and I must have done over two hundred shows together traveling in old Luxury. Alabama and Mississippi were hot in the summer, and it was a treat to crank up the generator and sleep in the cool air.

I almost died one night in the motorhome with Sheri. I was playing a gig for two nights in Sheffield, Alabama, and it was hot. The generator was running to power the air conditioner. In the middle of the night, I woke up feeling very disoriented. I got up and was all wobbly though I hadn't been drinking that hard. When I saw the cats, they had their noses to the door and were down on the lowest step at the bottom of the door. I knew something was wrong, so I opened the door, and the cats jumped out. I realized that carbon monoxide from the generator was poisoning us.

The next day was a nightmare for Sheri and me. The pain from the poisoning stayed with us for a while, but we survived it. I had to play that night, and I played one slow blues tune after another with the most agonizing pain I'd ever experienced during a four-hour gig. It was unbelievable, and something I'd never want to go through again. I don't know if I have a lower IQ or not because of it, but carbon monoxide poisoning is extremely painful.

Once in late June, Sheri and I were up in north Alabama, staying in Luxury while I played some gigs. We were coming back along the road from Moulton towards Birmingham, and, all of a sudden, I started feeling amorous. It was only me and my gal. I pulled over and while we were fooling around, the motor died. When we finished, I tried to crank the motor, which struggled to start, but finally did. Looking out the window I saw a light, which was odd since the road was so dark. I ran outside and looked underneath old Luxury to find the whole engine was on fire! Oh, my God! I ran back in and turned the engine off, but the fire was still burning. I screamed at Sheri to grab her cats and get out of the vehicle, as far away from it as she could. I was scrambling to get my guitar and get it outside. I grabbed a fire extinguisher and flipped open the tiny hood where you could change the oil. I started hosing the engine down, and it finally looked like I had gotten the fire out.

Just as I went back inside, old Luxury started herself! The starter turned over as I stood in the middle of the motorhome. It was like a scene from a horror movie. All I could think was that I was about to be standing in the middle of a huge explosion! There was still gas all over the place because the electric fuel pump had been pumping gas up and out of the carburetor. I knew if there was a spark, that'd be all she wrote. I ran back outside and reached into the hood to yank out the battery cable. It finally came off and old Luxury stopped. Thank God, that was the worst of it. What a night!

The day after the fire, I was supposed to catch a plane in Birmingham to fly to Portland with Johnny and his wife for the Rose City Blues Fest. That next morning, I walked to a little upholstery shop down the road from where Luxury burned up, and I called my friend Haz. I told him that I was broke down and needed to be on a plane in about six hours. "What am I gonna do?" I asked.

Haz said, "We'll call a tow truck and have 'em tow the motorhome to Norm's. Sheri can stay there and plug into the electricity, so she'll be all right for a week. When you get back, we'll get it towed over, and see what we can do to fix it."

Haz was a real lifesaver. Some friends are very valuable, especially at certain times in your life. Haz was that kind of friend. He had to completely rewire old Luxury to get her up and running again. He was such a champ and the best mechanic that anyone could know. He took his time with everything, and he made sure he did things right. He never stressed, or at least, he never showed it. I loved him to death!

Once, I had Luxury parked outside at Norm's while I partied late into the wee hours inside. I had played all night and was finally finished at about 7 o'clock in the morning. I was sitting at the bar drinking kamikazes with the boys when this big woman patted me on the shoulder and said, "Dance with me." She was huge, an Amazon.

I said, "No, no, no. I'm just drinking with the boys." A little while later, she patted me on the shoulder again and asked me to dance. Again, I said, "No." Then BB King's Thrill Is Gone came on the jukebox and she was back at it again; I finally gave in and it was a "big" mistake, no pun intended.

We were bouncing around the dance floor and I was drunk as a skunk. As we were dancing, I dipped her back once, and then again. On the third time I dipped her, my leg snapped and down we went, crashing to the floor! She landed right on top of me and her boobs flew out of her dress. Everybody was staring at me and my broken leg. Finally, I managed to get up and hopped back to the bar to drink another shot or two. I could feel the pain radiating up my leg and told my friends that I thought I'd broke my leg. They laughed it off and I hobbled back out to Luxury.

I couldn't walk at all the next day and a friend brought me a pair of crutches. I tried getting around on them for a couple of days, hoping it might be only a sprain. I wanted it to heal so I could get to Auburn to play a show. I remember how difficult it was trying to load my equipment while using a pair of crutches.

I did manage to do the show, and one of my fans was the head of the veterinary school at Auburn University. He said, "Kent, why don't you come in, and we'll x-ray you on the large animal table." I went in next morning and, sure enough, they spread me out on this table that they used for horses on and x-rayed me. I had a fractured leg and had to get a doctor to fix me up.

I hobbled around for six weeks with a cast on my leg, and still had it on when Johnny Shines, my brother, and I all piled into Luxury for a fishing trip up to the Smoky Mountains in Tennessee. I had a spot up there in the Tellico wilderness that I loved for stock rainbow and round brown trout fishing, and I knew Johnny would have a time. He was a little bit nervous up there in the mountains because a lot of those folks had never seen a Black man before. When we pulled into Tellico Plains for breakfast, Johnny was getting looks from all the local boys because I think they really hadn't seen a Black man in a long time.

We stopped at a bait shop, and I walked in while Johnny and my brother stayed in the motorhome. Sitting there inside was a barefoot guy in dungarees and a checked shirt. His head was a little bit bigger than most, and he was playing a Gibson banjo. Oh, my goodness, I couldn't believe it! This was straight out of the movie Deliverance. I thought that I should go get Johnny and film a whole thing of us jamming with this kid. I thought this was too good to be true, but I also thought it could really cause some problems for us. No Black people lived in this area, and a lot of them didn't even know what a Black person really even looked like. I decided to pass on this impromptu jam session. I don't know if I regret it or not, but it was one of those scenes that you could imagine in the movies, with the kid and the banjo in the bait shop in the Appalachian Mountains. I was a long-haired hippie boy and Johnny was a Black man. We'd have sat there playing and the footage would've been great, but I chickened out for the sake of our safety. Instead, we hit the mountains and caught lots of fish.

After Johnny passed away, I continued living in Luxury and running around with my third wife-to-be, Sheri. I loved my fishing, so we traveled out west and fished a lot, playing up and down the mountains from Montana to Wyoming to Idaho to Utah. I remember spending a couple of nights in a shop in Idaho Falls getting repairs done to the rear end of Luxury. That old motorhome saw many parking lots, transmission shops, and heavy truck repair shops. You name a place and I've probably lived there for a day, week, or a month. My journeys in old Luxury reflected the life of the bluesmen of that time.

I later sold Luxury in Georgia to a man named Hatfield, who claimed to be one of the heirs of Hatfield-McCoy fame. As far as I know, Luxury is still parked out in a field somewhere near Georgetown, Georgia.

11

Lazy Bill Lucas

Lazy Bill Lucas was an old, blind Black piano player who grew up in Wynne, Arkansas. I'm not sure if Bill was blind at birth or if something happened when he was quite young. He couldn't work in the fields and do the work that some kids were doing; he had to stay home and babysit the other kids in his family. He was one of the cool, blues piano players that migrated from the South and was part of the birth of the Chicago blues scene in the '40s and '50s.

At one point, Bill was playing with Sonny Boy Williams, who was one of the great blues harp players of the day. Sonny Boy Williams was stabbed to death with an ice pick on the streets of Chicago late one night. Lazy Bill was supposedly with him that night and it's my understanding that Bill left Chicago because it was so rough. He moved to Minneapolis and was playing around the Twin Cities area.

When my friends and I were 17 or 18, we used to go over to his house on Lake Street and hang out. We jammed with him and drank a bunch of cheap beer that he kept locked in a small closet. The closet was stacked from top to bottom with cases of Fox Deluxe beer. It was the cheapest beer you could buy, and Bill used to pay about $5.00 for a case of 24. He was a big fan of the brandy too.

Lazy Bill was always so excited to see us young guys coming. Actually, "see" is poor word choice—after all, he was blind! Anyway, he loved people that loved blues music and he was happy when we were there. At that time, we were only beginning to learn about blues music, so Bill was kind of our godfather. I saw Bill play many times in many different situations. He usually played solo, but he did have some times when he'd have a band playing with him. Many times it was with friends of ours or with us. He also did a few overseas tours.

Though Bill wasn't totally blind, the impairment was enough that he was considered legally blind. He could see enough to move around, but details were tough for him. He smoked these extra-long cigarettes because he didn't want to burn himself when he was lighting them.

While Lazy Bill was best known for his blues piano playing, he played a lot of classics too. He would do songs like Blueberry Hill and some Ray Charles' songs. He took on a friend of mine, Tommy Burns, as a harmonica player. At that time, Bill was maybe in his late 50s or early 60s. To us younger guys, he always seemed older than he really was. Even though we thought he was ancient, we loved to hang out with him.

I was with Bill one night on Lake Minnetonka. He was doing a show with Tommy, and he started complaining about not feeling well. So, I stepped in and started playing in place of him so that he could relax and rest. I finished up the show, and we went back to Minneapolis. We came to find out the next day that old Bill had had a heart attack and passed away that night.

Bill was to be buried in Chicago, but before his body was shipped there, we had a big wake. Baby Doo Caston was another local musician who lived in Minneapolis, and he hosted the wake. I remember Baby Doo saying that he regretted not sticking with the blues because Bill was so adored and had so many fans around the world. Baby Doo had branched out from the blues and started playing more contemporary music. Baby Doo had traveled with Willie Dixon back in the '30s and '40s. They did a lot of contemporary music at the time when the Ink Spots were famous. When he moved to Minneapolis, Baby Doo played in big, fancy hotels. He was a piano player and rarely did any blues shows. He seemed to have some regrets about not being true to the blues music that he loved so much.

Later that night, after the wake, we had a big celebration for Bill. We all jammed together, celebrating Bill's legacy. While we were celebrating, a huge blizzard blew into town. It was one of the worst snowstorms I'd ever experienced. The snow was blowing and drifting and the roads were really dangerous. It was a disaster trying to leave the club and the drive home was a nightmare! About five miles from my house, it got so bad that I finally had to get off the road. I tried to get out and walk, but the whiteout made it difficult to judge direction, so I guided by looking at the Metrodome—the big stadium where the Vikings and Twins played back then. I fell once and lost my keys, so when I eventually made it home, I had to break in. Whenever I think about Bill's passing, I always remember the crazy storm that damn near killed me too, so I've always called it the Lazy Bill Blizzard of 1982.

That was the end of old Lazy Bill Lucas, another of the old-time blues players who had a huge influence on me as a young musician. What a great bluesman and great guy.

12

Howlin' Wolf in Concert

Howlin' Wolf's given name was Chester Burnett. I believe that I first saw him in 1969 at the Cedar Theater in Minneapolis where he was doing a concert. Tickets were on sale, but I couldn't afford to buy one.

Even without a ticket, I went down to the theater and hung around the stage door, hoping I might get a little glimpse of the great Howlin' Wolf. Luckily, there was a crack in the door and I was able see him a little as he stood on stage singing his blues. I continued to hang around and hoped the stage manager or one of the sound men would come to take a break and open the door. That way, I could sneak in to stand in the wings and watch old Wolf. Sadly, that didn't happen. But at the end of the show, there were lots of people standing around outside where I was, so they opened the doors and let everybody in for the encore. We got to see him briefly on stage that night and I remember noticing that the audience was just about all white people who were close to my age.

I saw him again in August 1970, at the Ann Arbor Blues Fest. There were all kinds of cool blues cats there over three days at the Otis Spann Memorial Field. Ten thousand of us white boys partied with just about every cool blues cat that was alive.

Howlin' Wolf closed out the show on Friday night. He rode a motorcycle onto the stage, then he jumped off this little bike and started howling and singing his blues. The crowd went crazy! He turned his hat sideways and was goofing around, and then he dangled his microphone down by his crotch and swung it around. He was quite the showman and had a ton of charisma.

A little later that night, we worked our way into Ann Arbor to this small bar where I used to play. It was called Mr. Flood's Party, and sitting there onstage was the great Howlin' Wolf. Mississippi Fred McDowell was sitting next to him and behind, a skinny little Johnny Winter stood in the back of this tiny stage. It was really strange to see Howlin' Wolf there because he'd just been out onstage in front of all these white boys at this big festival. Now he was in this little bar blowing his harp and singing his blues.

I thought, "Wow, why would he do that?" The only thing I could come up with was that he was doing it because this was where he felt most comfortable. He obviously got paid well for the festival, had all the drinks he wanted and about 10,000 adoring fans. Yet, he was one of those late-night blues cats that loved getting in a little spot and just hunkering down and laying the blues on the audience. He didn't necessarily need a big show. I felt proud because I had been on that stage a month earlier, playing my first blues road trip.

One of the other things I remember from that Ann Arbor Fest is this woman that was seductively snake dancing all afternoon and evening in front of the different cats that were playing. She was getting these guys all excited. She danced by Albert King, Freddy King, Mighty Joe Young, and others I can't remember. When Howlin' Wolf came out to do his show, she was still twisting and snaking around the stage. For Wolf's show, there was this big, elevated chair that looked like a throne. Howlin' Wolf was singing and playing, and as he got up in that chair, the woman was snake dancing around him. She was wiggling on the edge of the stage. Wolf took the microphone and said to the woman, "Be gone! I got a woman at home that feeds me with a gold spoon." With that, the dancer snaked her way right off the stage. Wolf wasn't having any of that stuff during his show.

13

More on Europe

It wasn't until 1992 that I started traveling and performing overseas. I started in Switzerland, playing the blues at the Bop Festival in Lugano. Norman Hewitt ran the festival and was a huge blues fan, so it leaned heavily on blues cats. He brought some pretty cool musicians in to play. Norman (who sadly passed away in 2017) was a great guy who was seriously into the blues and knew a lot about it.

During the '90s, I played often in France and Italy and a little in Germany, Belgium, and Holland. The European scene appeared to center on traditional Black blues artists, so I had to really step it up a notch. I felt like I needed to prove myself as far as performing and having any credentials that were valid for them. I did make some great connections with blues fans and made friends in those places. I did well in Italy and would try to arrange gigs in France and Germany. The latter two countries seemed very disjointed; nobody had a handle on booking for a whole country, so it was always a challenge to get enough bookings. Some of the countries didn't have much going on early in the week, so it was also difficult to fill in enough dates.

I did some playing in Sweden, but Norway was the place to go! There was a very vibrant and growing blues scene when I first went there in the early '90s and it blossomed into all kinds of blues clubs. It really became a desirable touring area for me. I did many tours in Norway, running up and down those roads once or twice a year during the mid-'90s and into the 2000s. I still tour in Scandinavia but not as much as I used to. They still have some fabulous blues festivals every year, and when I have the opportunity, I go and perform. I've made many Norwegian friends over the years.

Britain is, and has been, a staunch supporter of the blues. The people of Britain have been following blues music since the '50s when they brought over all the country and Chicago blues artists that they could get their hands on. The scene flourished and is still thriving in the UK. It's one of their main musical genres.

There are still many good players and entertainers performing in Britain; some of the old dogs are still around doing their blues shows. For many years, the radio had Paul Jones' blues show on Monday night and people listened to it religiously. Many of the great guitarists like Eric Clapton, Jimmy Page, Jeff Beck, and Keith Richards loved the blues. Those guys focused on learning how to play it, and then incorporated blues into their rock 'n' roll. Britain just has so many blues festivals and the fans to support them.

Ireland is beautiful country, but it's more traditional about music. Although they're not as focused on the blues as the Brits, they do have some great blues festivals and I was fortunate to play there some. The Guinness Blues Festival in Dublin was quite exciting and prestigious. I got to drink Guinness with the president of the company at the brewery in Dublin. Monaghan in the north has a great festival every year, and I performed there from time to time. Almost everyone in Ireland can play an instrument and they're good at evaluating the way you perform. Once you get going, they can tell whether there's any authenticity to your playing because they're so talented musically. Northern Ireland has a thriving music scene, but it's also not so interested in blues. When I visited Ireland, I remember the friction between the Catholics and the Protestants. We actually crossed from Ireland into Northern Ireland about the time of the peace accord and the cease fire. There was barbed wire and spotlights everywhere at the border. It looked like one of those border crossings in Berlin, Germany, during the Cold War, and it was very unnerving.

All in all, my gigs abroad have really given me wonderful memories. I've formed so many special friendships over the years that I wouldn't trade my time traveling and playing in Europe for anything.

14

The Women in My Life

I've certainly talked about the women in my life throughout the book, but they deserve a chapter devoted just to them. From an early age, I was attracted to females, and like most kids, always fancied a certain girl in my class. I wanted to be in a relationship with a girl; specifically, I wanted to be in a relationship with a pretty girl. I don't know why I was so obsessed with looks. I guess maybe it was because I grew up in that era of Playboy showcasing a woman with a beautiful body and a beautiful face. Growing up, those were the characteristics I valued in women. Right or wrong, it's just the way it was.

My exposure to Playboy came early. As kids, we would go to the drugstore to stand in the magazine section to try and get our hands on copies. We were thrilled to get a glimpse of those beautiful naked bodies. Sometimes the bosses would come by, and we'd get busted for looking.

Being stimulated by a picture of a naked body was one

thing. Meeting a real, live, beautiful woman was another. When I was growing up, relationships I had were few and far between. I don't know if I was too shy or if the girls just weren't interested, but I do know that in my early teens, there was lots of lust but not much action. I didn't have an actual relationship until my mid-teens. The group I hung out with were considered the rebels in our town and our girls weren't interested in rebels. We moved to the next city, however, and found relationships there. I had a couple of girlfriends from the next town and that lasted until I graduated and moved out of the house.

Once I had a bit of freedom, life became about playing music and meeting girls. Different relationships formed. Some were short and only lasted overnight; I guess those one-night stands were a part of the music scene. Musicians like me, who moved around a lot and weren't interested in settling down, didn't exactly encourage anything long term.

Finally, I met a little gal from my hometown, and we got pretty serious to the point where I thought maybe she would be the one for me. I proposed marriage and bought her a ring. Unfortunately, I had to go to Ohio to play in a band for the winter and leave my fiancée behind. Of course, she found somebody else, and when I came back, it was over between us. Maybe that was a prelude to my relationships for the future.

I resumed playing the music, running the roads, and having one-night stands with women. Then, in the mid-'70s, I met a beautiful gal and we became close. She didn't move in with me, but we spent a lot of time together. She was a local girl who really liked the music I played. Her name was Candy, and she was good looking and very sexual. She was also a nurse and quite intelligent. I recall one cute little story that happened with Candy and Boogie Woogie Red, the piano player that our band backed up. Red was from Detroit, and one night when he was playing, Candy was standing in the front of the audience. She wasn't giving him the eye but was being happy and bouncy and smiley and encouraging. He stopped and said girl, "What's your name?"

"Candy," she answered. He reached into his pocket, dug out a quarter, flipped it to her and said, "Candy, I'm the Candy wrapper." She got a big laugh out of that, and so did I. I liked Candy, but she got a little too possessive and I eventually broke up with her.

Then in 1977, I met my first ex-wife to be. Again, I was playing music, and noticed this sweet little gal in the audience. I invited her home, and the next thing I knew, we were riding the roads together. Her name was Greta and she was wonderful: smart, artsy, and a great dancer. Her moves were incredible; she felt the music and could dance in an improvisational way, like poetry in motion. We went down to Texas and lived in my van and a big UPS truck while I played music there. We were starving to death in Texas, so we moved back north, and I started working as a chef. We had a little hideout, and things were good for a while. Then she said, "Kent, my parents, grandparents, and everyone else are bugging me to get married. We're living together, and they're very religious. So, what do you think? Will you marry me?"

I cared for Greta very much and didn't want to lose her, so I agreed to marry her. It worked out fine for a while. She put up with my crap although I was very immature, demanding, boyish, and always wanting my way. Up north, we worked for my brother at his resort for three years. We traveled in the winters and even went as far as Central America, where we spent three months running the roads down there. We had some great times together, but she could see that I was too immature. I would get angry when I drank too much and she eventually decided that she had to move on; I guess you could say she reached her breaking point. We ended that marriage in the early '80s. Greta was one of the best, a real angel. I had totally screwed that relationship up and wanted to move on after the devastation of getting divorced.

Lisa was marriage number two, a fiery redhead from Alabama. We first met down on the Gulf Coast when I was playing gigs there for the first time. In 1983, I played the Flora-Bama Lounge, a popular roadhouse, and she was a cute little redhead who tended bar and waited tables. She gave me the eye, and the next thing I knew, we'd hooked up. She was quite a character who played all sides against the middle to get what she wanted.

Lisa partied hard, taking lots of barbiturates and drinking a ton; she loved her vodka. We started traveling together. She came with me on my first trip to Key West and we lived in the old Caddy. Easter was the official end of the season down in the Keys, so we shot off to the Virgin Islands. One night while down there, she backed me up against the wall and said, "Kent, you've gotta marry me, or I'm leaving." I fell for it; we were married by a judge on the island of St. Thomas.

One of the trips back to Key West had me playing ten shows a week, and I found out Lisa was cheating on me. We split up, and she went back to Alabama. She was extremely beautiful; she looked kind of like Ann-Margaret with wonderful red hair and a great body. She just had this light in her that everyone could see.

Lisa loved animals and had a special quality when it came to nurturing those critters. We had all kinds of little wild animal pets from squirrels to birds. We even had a baby beaver that she raised. She was quite a gal, and I tried to get back together with her after her little adulterous moments, but some ass from Louisiana moved in on me. He was a bridge builder, and he took over. He had the money she liked, as well as the power. So, that was it. I moved on from there, and it took some years before we got divorced, which was due in part to my meeting my third wife, Sheri.

Sheri was a beautiful blonde that I met while performing at the Smithsonian Festival of Folklife in D.C. in 1991. She was in the audience during the shows and at the evening sessions at the hotel where the workers and the performers would gather for dinner every evening. There'd be some musical entertainment, so it was kind of a party every evening. When she showed up, I made my move. The next thing I knew, she was taking me to a hotel and paying for it all with her credit card.

Sheri was extremely independent, gorgeous, and smart. We hooked up after the festival, and I invited her up to Minnesota to hang out with me. She came up from Virginia, where she'd been staying with relatives. We ran the roads of Minnesota in my motorhome for two or three wonderful weeks. We saw the northern lights, visited the wild lakes, and partied hard before she left and went back to Virginia.

I was crazy about Sheri. She lived in Texas, where she was going to school. I convinced her to come and live with me in my motorhome in Alabama in the parking lot of the late-night bar, Norm's. She agreed and brought her little Toyota along with some other possessions, including two kitty cats. We moved in together and started running the roads in the motorhome, always coming back to Norm's for our hangout. We eventually moved out to a campground on Oak Mountain, outside of Birmingham. It was beautiful there and ideal for us since we traveled so much. You could rent a spot on a monthly basis.

We ran back and forth across America, down to the Gulf of Mexico, up to Minnesota, and traveled out west a couple of times. I started going overseas after Johnny Shines died, which enabled me to save some cash. I bought a big F350 Ford Dually and a 28-foot travel trailer to go on the back, so we had quite the rig when we were traveling. We had lots of space, and it was quite luxurious.

At some point, Sheri decided we needed to get married. I did not want to lose this beautiful blonde, so I agreed and off to Opelika, Alabama, we went to find a judge. We decided that since I was able to go overseas and earn good cash, we should start looking for some land to buy. We searched all over Alabama, and there wasn't much to be found that was in our price range, which was low. We'd been looking for a year or so when we found a little spot on Lake Eufaula on the Georgia side of the lake, where prices were much lower. It had seventy-five feet of waterfront in a subdivision that had a few houses, but most lots had double trailers stuck together and built around, so they looked like houses. We got a spot there at Bonaparte's Retreat where I was hoping to live happily ever after. This place on Lake Eufaula was a major accomplishment for me because I lived on the road for so many years. I was always on the move with no phone, no TV, and no address.

I always wanted to live on the water, so it was a major deal for me to be able to buy a little piece of heaven on a beautiful lake filled with big-mouth bass. I was very excited, and I decided I was going to build a small studio out in the back, overlooking the lake. I'd have my inspiration for recording and a place to hang out that had a beautiful view. In front of the house was a boat in the lake at our dock.

Well, my beautiful blonde gal appeared to be in love with me and our new place, but then, there was a run-in with the neighbors. Sheri decided we needed to look elsewhere for a place, so we started looking around for land. Ten miles down the lake, we found a couple of undeveloped lots. I was in love and agreed to go for it, so we bought the lots and cleared a few trees off one of them so we could build. I built a big post-and-beam 2,800-square foot house. This is where we lived when we adopted Sheri's niece's son, Miles. He is the joy of my life.

In 2006, Sheri decided that she wasn't in love with me and had never been in love with me. After telling her we'd better call it quits, I asked what was going to happen with Miles, who was about four at the time. She asked if I would take him in and I did, becoming his primary caregiver. Whenever I went overseas to perform, Miles would stay with Sheri, who agreed to look after him when I was gone.

When our divorce was finalized, all the property and bills became mine. I carried on that way for a year or so, and then met my future fourth wife, Sarah, a beautiful blonde from Britain. In my autumn tour of 2007, I was performing at the Jam House in Birmingham, England. This beautiful blonde came up and started looking at the CDs I had for sale. She purchased a couple of them, and I chatted with her a little. She was incredibly gorgeous and was the top lap dancer in a place called The Spearmint Rhino. I was only dreaming of a connection, when low and behold, she and a friend, another stripper, showed up at one of my gigs at The Flowerpot. My friend Andy gave Sarah a schedule and invited her to come to a show that he was putting on down the road, and I was delighted when she showed up again. Three times lucky! Later that night, I asked her where the party was. She said they were heading back to her flat and invited me to come along—an opportunity I wasn't about to turn down. The next thing I knew, I was in a relationship with this gorgeous, blonde lap dancer.

One thing led to another, and I invited Sarah to come with me to tour Scotland. We had a great time there and I invited her and her son to come visit me in America later in the year when I got home from touring. They came around Thanksgiving. We first went to New Orleans, and then to the Flora-Bama to do some shows at the Songwriter Festival.

My 5-year-old son, Miles, came onstage and played with me on his little acoustic guitar for about 30 minutes. The crowd loved him! Women were throwing jewelry at Miles' feet and the guys were throwing cash to him.

Sarah came and spent Christmas with me, which was fabulous. We eventually got married, and as usual, things started falling apart at some point. When you start a relationship, it's all exciting and new. Then, the new wears off and you start making compromises. If you feel that things aren't quite equitable, you either shut up or make a fuss. Things with us worked out in such a way that it was off to the lawyers to get another divorce decree written up.

My son, Miles, is a guitar boy, musically gifted and a great kid. Like all teenagers, he has his challenges, but he seems to be coping okay with them. I'm very proud of him, and he's never caused me a bit of trouble. I have the typical parental concerns about raising him right and helping him make it to adulthood.

If a future fifth wife appears on the horizon, we will deal with that as it comes. For now, it's about time to head to the ramp, put the boat in and get some of those largemouth bass and maybe a dozen crappies for dinner. Life goes on at home and on the road as I continue making my music.

In closing, we all need to lift our glasses and toast all the great bluesmen and women who made the blues what it is. I certainly have them to thank for my career, and for all of the music that they've brought into my life.

BLUES FOREVER

www.ingramcontent.com/pod-product-compliance
Lightning Source LLC
Chambersburg PA
CBHW062111080426
42734CB00012B/2829